Breads of Many Lands

Breads of Many Lands

Florence Laffal

GALLERY PRESS   ESSEX   CONNECTICUT

Library of Congress Catalog Card Number 73-94308

ISBN 0-913622-01-X

Printed in the United States of America
by Halliday Lithograph Corporation
West Hanover, Massachusetts 02339

A loaf of bread, the walrus said,
Is what we chiefly need:
Pepper and vinegar besides
Are very good indeed.
                    -Lewis Carroll
              Through the Looking Glass

Contents

INTRODUCTION

My favorite old-country cook's recipe for blintzes went something like this: "put in enough flour so it looks just right'", and add water "about the size of an egg". I thought then that cookbooks would have the real recipes, formulas with precise, foolproof measurements. That was 20 years ago.

There are in fact many cookbooks with precise formulas, and I have learned a great deal from them. But the real fun of baking comes when the cook learns to appreciate the notion of adding enough flour so that it "looks just right" (and feels just right, too), and allows herself a bit of free wheeling. After all, a recipe tasting "just right" to you may be lacking salt or be too pungent for someone else. With bread baking especially, exact measurements are impossible. Yeasted dough is affected by heat, moisture, sugar, altitude and no doubt by the personality and mood of the baker. If too much flour gets into the batter, the bread may be heavy and stiff. If too little goes in, the bread will not hold up as well and you'll wind up with a flat bread. You will still have a bread, just a different kind. It is difficult to make a serious mistake in baking bread. Errors inevitably turn into inventions.

My idea in baking is never to make a thing twice in exactly the same way. Use cookbooks as guides (this one as well), and create the rest of the way. Your rewards will be plentiful. Your family and friends will enjoy the smells and taste of homemade bread and you the extra pleasure of having baked it.

The recipes in *BREADS OF MANY LANDS* follow a unique format. Ingredients are listed first so that they may be assembled and be at hand when preparation of the bread begins. Each phase in the process is then shown distinctly from the others on the page. The major phases in bread baking are *LEAVENING, BATTER, DOUGH, KNEADING, RISING, BAKING* and *SERVING* (although not all recipes go through exactly the same phases). Segmenting the recipes in this way has two advantages: it is easier to find your place when you are returning for the next step, and after doing a few of the recipes you will know the general process of bread baking by heart.

Many bread books multiply recipes by simply repeating basic recipes with minor variations and new names. It makes more sense to present the basic recipe which distinguishes a particular type of bread from other breads. Variations may be achieved in many ways.

Take the recipe for WHITE BREAD (page 27). If 3 of the 6 cups of white flour are replaced with 3 cups of whole wheat flour, you get a WHOLE WHEAT BREAD. If 3 cups of rye flour replace 3 cups of white, you get a RYE BREAD. Substitute 1 cup each of whole wheat, graham and soy flour for 3 cups of white, to produce a HIGH PROTEIN BREAD. To make an HERB BREAD from the white bread recipe, add a couple of teaspoons of mixed herbs such as chives, basil, summer savory, poppy seeds, anise.

White bread may be made richer by introducing 1 or 2 eggs (don't over-do it). Simply remember to use ¼ cup less liquid for each egg. If more sweetening or honey is added along with eggs, you begin to get a COFFEE CAKE. Coffee cakes and sweet rolls have a higher proportion of yeast to flour than does bread, so to turn the white bread recipe completely into a coffee cake recipe, add one more package of yeast. The coffee cake recipe may now be changed into a HOLIDAY BREAD recipe by adding candied fruits, nuts, liqueur, icing or any other sweetener and decoration.

And so on with other transformations and new creations, starting from the basic white bread recipe!

Suggestions for shaping breads are given in most recipes. But there is no need to be bound strictly by the instructions. Dough is malleable and can become a sculptural medium in creative hands. Make abstract shapes, braids, swirls, twists, animals, humans, trees, flowers. Your breads should be conversation pieces.

Try whatever pleases you. Be an experimenter, be an artist while you are baking.

THE QUIET REVOLUTION

The bread of prehistoric man is believed to have been flat and unleavened, baked over hot stones. The discovery of leavening was probably accidental: batter left in the hot sun would attract wild yeast from the air and become fermented. The Greek historian Herodotus tells of Egyptian bread baking in the 5th century B.C. According to his account the Egyptians used clay brick ovens and were familiar with the use of leavening in bread.

The Greeks themselves prepared many different types of breads, one of the most popular being a flat bread baked over coals and rolled up like a scroll. Remains of home and public bakeries have been found in the ruins of Pompeii, and also carbonized breads which were flat, round and scored into wedges - like the pizza of today!

In many lands breads are still baked by primitive methods. In India and Nepal the chapatty is made as in olden time by patting out the dough with the hands. The nomadic tribes of Iran bake a similar unleavened bread over hot stones, and even the modern leavened breads of Iran are baked over hot pebbles. The Mexican tortilla, truly a primitive bread, is eagerly devoured today (to observe the local shops in Mexico City on a Saturday night) by poor and well-to-do alike.

In the United States bread has been largely made of bleached flour, machine mixed, machine baked and wrapped. Most of the natural nutrients have been taken out of the wheat in the course of milling and bleaching the flour, in order to present a snow-white bread of esthetic appearance. Then, to compensate for the depredation, artificial enrichment has been put back in.

People are returning to old methods and rediscovering the value of natural foods - a quiet revolution! There is nothing like the smell of bread baking in the kitchen to give the feel of HOME. Bread baking is basic. The flour milled from the wheat and formed into a dough, is mixed with a yeast plant that burgeons in warm water. The kneading, the rising, the shaping, the baking, all have a natural rhythm - they cannot be rushed.

So plan on a baking day and make several breads at once. Between the risings or during the baking, other work may be scheduled. Keep some of the breads for a week or so in plastic wrappings; freeze others for future use. But be sure to have one fresh for the table that very night.

INGREDIENTS

SUGAR, HONEY AND MAPLE SYRUP

In *BREADS OF MANY LANDS* the choice, wherever possible, has been for wholesome, nutritive ingredients in preference to the over-processed foods generally called for in standard recipes. Honey and maple syrup are recommended in place of refined sugar. Each of these not only provides the necessary sweetening, but also imparts an entirely new flavor of its own to sweet breads, rolls and muffins. Most cookbooks persist in emphasizing sugar, despite common knowledge of the harmful effects of sugar on teeth and on the health in general.

Enough sugar is present in flour starch to activate the yeast in a bread dough. Adding sugar to most recipes of French, Italian or Cuban breads does nothing but mask the authentic flavor of the original. However, it would not do always to omit sugar. A French brioche, for example, would lose its opulent flavor without sugar.

YEAST

Yeast comes dry in a package or fresh, compressed in a small cake. Dry yeast is called for in *BREADS OF MANY LANDS*, but compressed yeast may be used if available. Water temperature for dry yeast is about 110° (very warm but not hot), whereas fresh yeast needs 80°- 90° (lukewarm).

UNBLEACHED WHITE FLOUR

Unbleached white flour is the best choice of the white flours available. Although not recommended, bleached white flour may be used as a substitute. Flour is sifted for some holiday and coffee breads to a- chieve a fine-grained quality in the product.

WHOLE WHEAT FLOUR

Whole wheat flour, containing more of the bran of the wheat, is more nutritious and more glutenous than white flour. An all wheat dough would be quite sticky and difficult to knead, so whole wheat bread recipes call for part white flour.

RYE FLOUR

Rye flour is less glutenous and is coarser grained than wheat flour. Rye flour is responsible for the familiar hearty texture in rye breads and rolls. It is therefore never sifted.

CORN MEAL

Corn meal is grainy and lacks gluten. It is often combined with white flour to provide both cohesiveness and improved taste.

ROLLED OATS

Rolled oats make a tasty addition in white bread, and also provide good nutrition. Rolled oats are often used in combination with honey or molasses.

BARLEY FLOUR	Pan roasted barley flour gives a chewiness and nutlike flavor to bread, somewhat unfamiliar to western taste.
SOY FLOUR	Substitute ¼ cup of soy flour for ¼ cup of white flour to make a protein rich bread.
SPROUTED WHEAT OR BEANS	Try some sprouted wheat or sprouted beans for a fresh garden flavor in bread. Wheat berries or mung beans are especially tasty. Stir fry before adding them to the recipe.
EGGS	Many recipes for cakes and breads are brimming with eggs. Because of the high cholesterol content in eggs, *BREADS OF MANY LANDS* uses them in moderation. There is little difference in taste if 2 eggs are used instead of 3, as long as the proper balance is maintained between wet and dry ingredients. Omit an egg and add ¼ cup water or milk.
MILK	Fresh or dry milk may be used, either whole or skim. Whole milk yields a richer product.
OIL	Use a pure vegetable oil which has no additives, such as peanut oil. If a shortening such as spry is used instead of oil, add proportionately more water or milk.
BUTTER	Butter should be unsalted or lightly salted. Margarine may be used instead of butter.

Most of the ingredients described above may be purchased in the super-market. Barley flour, soy flour, wheat berries and mung beans may be gotten at an organic food store.

Directions for yeasted breads are for the straight dough method (as opposed to the sourdough or sponge method), in which all ingredients are mixed together step by step to form a dough before kneading and rising. An important point to remember about yeasted bread recipes is that the amount of flour used may actually be ½ cup more or less than prescribed. Bear in mind that about ½ cup flour must be reserved for sprinkling on the kneading surface, to be absorbed in the dough during the kneading.

LEAVENING

Begin yeasted breads by dissolving the yeast (leavening) in warm water and allowing the solution to stand for 5 minutes. Water should be warm but not hot (110°).

BATTER

About half the flour is beaten vigorously into the dissolved yeast along with warm milk or water to form a smooth batter. More flour is added to the batter, a little at a time, while working it actively with a paddle.

DOUGH

"Batter flows, dough doesn't." This is about as good a distinction between batter and dough as any. When the batter no longer sticks to the sides of the bowl and is workable with the hands, it has become a dough. The dough is turned out onto a lightly floured surface such as a board or a formica top, and the kneading begins.

KNEADING

Flour on the kneading surface will be absorbed as part of the total amount of flour in the dough. Add a little more flour if the dough tends to stick. It is important to knead the dough thoroughly. With the heels of the hands press down and away from you into the ball of dough. Give the dough a ¼ turn clockwise, then fold the dough toward the center. Give the dough a few hits with the hands as though you were beating a rug. Continue to press, turn and fold. The more you knead, the more elastic the dough will become, and the spongier the bread. Find your own rhythm and keep at it for about 10 minutes or until the dough

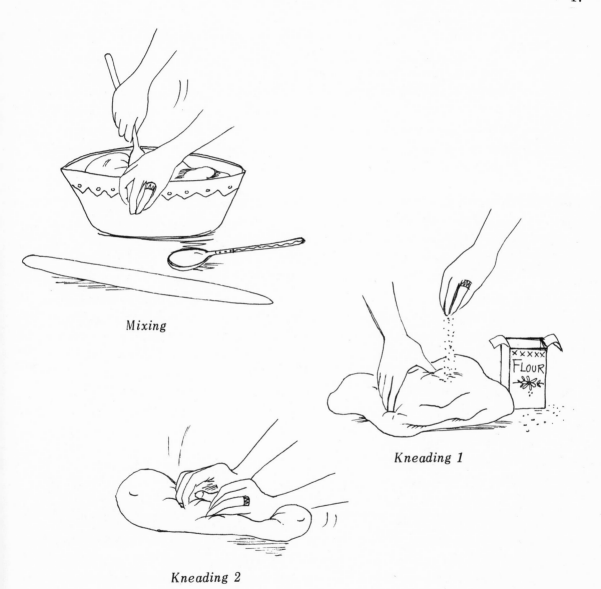

Mixing

Kneading 1

Kneading 2

Risen Dough

Punching Dough

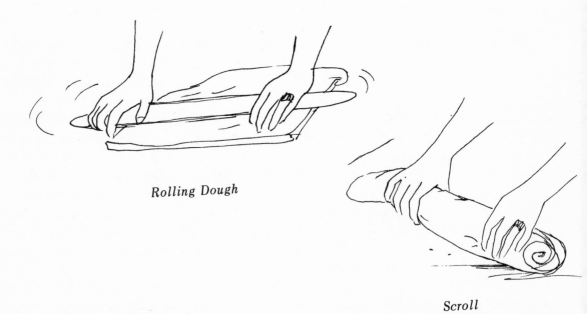

Rolling Dough

Scroll

is really smooth and elastic. It will require a bit of elbow grease, but the product will be well worth the effort. If you are unsure whether or not the dough has had the proper kneading, give it a few more rounds. Better to knead too much than too little.

As an alternative to kneading, some French bakers hit the dough against the board about 100 times. Try this technique for a French bread. It is quite exhausting!

RISING   The kneaded dough is put into a greased bowl and turned once to grease the top. The bowl is covered with waxed paper and a towel and set in a warm place for rising. A warm place may be the oven heated for 3 minutes at 200°, the oven with a shallow pan of boiling water on the bottom shelf, the top of a warm stove away from drafts.

The dough is allowed to rise about 1½ hours or until it doubles in bulk. Many things affect the rising of the dough: the atmosphere of the room, geographic altitude, proportion of water to flour in the dough, the manner in which the dough was kneaded, even the mood of the baker. It is well to keep an eye on the dough and make your own judgment of the rising. Push your index finger into the surface of the risen dough. If the impression remains, the rising is finished. If the impression disappears quickly, allow the dough to rise a bit more. Of one thing there can be no doubt, no two baking days will be exactly the same. When the dough is fully risen punch it down. The punching down may be done with hand or fist, or by poking holes through the surface with a sharp knife to allow air to escape. The dough will recede, but not to its original size.

SHAPING   The best way to shape a bread is to roll the dough out to a ½" thick rectangle, almost square, then roll it up like a scroll. From this point there are many options. The dough may be smoothed into a greased bread pan, formed into a dome for a round bread, or pulled out long and tapered at the ends for a French style bread. Always have edges of the dough on the bottom and smooth side on top.

Where the recipe calls for special shapes such as braids, cloverleaves and folded triangles, follow the instructions carefully.

SECOND RISING   The shaped bread is covered again and put into a warm place for its second rising. Thirty or 40 minutes will generally do.

BAKING   Preheat your oven to the temperature recommended by the recipe before putting in the bread. Ovens vary greatly and only through trial and error will you discover how your own oven performs. If your bread seems to be browning very rapidly, turn the oven down by 10° for the remainder of the baking time. Make a note of such discrepancies on the recipe. If your oven persists in browning fast, use a 10° lower temperature for all recipes. By and large, electric ovens heat more rapidly than gas ovens.

CRUSTS   For ryes, pumpernickels and sourdoughs, a pan of boiling water beneath the bread makes a crusty bread. For Cuban bread and oil rolls, ice water brushed on top makes for a shiny, crispy crust. For sweet doughs, challah and bagels, egg or egg yolk mixed with water or milk and brushed on top gives a golden glisten. For white bread, oatmeal bread and soft rolls, butter provides a soft, golden crust.

SOURDOUGH BREADS

At one time "soured" or fermented dough alone was used to make bread rise. Now that commercial yeasts are readily available as leavening, sourdough is used mainly for its taste. The name *Sourdough* was given to prospectors in Canada and Alaska because they habitually carried with them a lump of sour dough for use in baking bread. European bakers migrating to America would also take such a lump of dough with them.

Don't be frightened away from sourdough baking because of the length of time required. Once you get the hang of it sourdough bread is really simple to prepare. The tastiest French breads and the very best rye breads may be made from the same sourdough starter. If you keep a jar of starter in your refrigerator you can have a week of some of the most delicious tasting breads, pancakes and biscuits you've ever had. Sourdough breads may also be put away in the freezer for future use.

Sourdough recipes follow the format for yeasted breads except for the initial *LEAVENING* and *BATTER* phases. First of all a sourdough starter is prepared and left to ferment overnight or longer. The next day yeast and batter are added to the starter, forming sponge I which is allowed to ferment for several hours. Sponge I will rise for about 2½ hours, then fall. More yeast and batter are added to sponge I, and the new preparation (sponge II) is again left to ferment for several hours. Additional flour and other ingredients as called for, are added to sponge II to make a dough, and the recipe continues with *KNEADING, RISING* and so on as in yeasted breads.

SOURDOUGH STARTER Made from flour, water and yeast or from potatoes, water and yeast. The starter is left to ferment for at least one overnight.

SPONGE I Yeast, flour and water are added to the starter, and the mixture is set aside to ferment for about 4 hours. The sponge will rise and fall during the fermentation.

SPONGE II A second sponge is prepared by adding more yeast, flour and water to sponge I and allowing the mixture to ferment.

DOUGH   Add flour and other ingredients which may be called for in the recipe to sponge II to form a dough workable with the hands.

Now proceed with the remaining phases of bread preparation (*KNEADING, RISING, SHAPING, BAKING*) as for yeasted breads.

QUICK BREADS

As the name implies, quick bread is prepared rather quickly and unlike a yeasted bread does not require time for risings. Quick breads are usually prepared with a leavening either of baking powder or baking soda, and all of the rising takes place during baking. They are often made from a batter spooned or poured directly into a baking pan. Recipes for quick breads are short, since such phases as *KNEADING* and *RISING* are eliminated.

BATTER   In a quick bread such as a muffin, the batter is formed by mixing the wet ingredients into the dry ingredients all at once. Some quick breads like popovers require beating for a few minutes with an egg beater to make a light, airy batter. Few quick breads require extended mixing.

SHAPING   For most quick breads, shaping simply amounts to pouring the batter into a pan. The few quick breads that require a dough (baklawah, strudel) will have special directions in the recipe.

BAKING   Baking time for quick breads is normally from 20 to 40 minutes.

Flat breads of different lands are basically quite similar, being made simply of flour or corn meal mixed with water. The Indian chapatty, the Persian nane saj and the desert matzoh are made of wheat flour; the Mexican tortilla is made of corn meal. The dough is shaped into a ball, patted out flat and round, and baked on a metal plate or on hot stones. Tibetan barley balls, Nigerian agidi and Tibetan bread are in the flat bread family, although differing in shape and preparation.

INGREDIENTS   Corn meal or wheat flour and warm water are the essential ingredients Butter is used in Indian parathas, and matzohs may be made with eggs.

DOUGH   Mixing of the dough is generally an all in one process, the water being mixed quickly with the flour.

KNEADING   There is a short kneading of the dough, not as extensive as in yeasted breads. The dough is then covered with a damp cloth and set aside to rest for about 30 minutes.

SHAPING   The dough is shaped by patting or rolling out thin, flat and round. Matzohs are traditionally made square.

BAKING   Flat breads are baked quickly, for no more than 2 or 3 minutes. The chapatty, the tortilla and the matzoh are baked on a skillet. Persian nane saj is made on a convex metal plate. Indian puri is deep fried in a concave pan like a small wock.

SERVING   Flat breads are often filled with diced meat and vegetables to make the main dish of a meal.

Pancakes are thin breads made by frying batter in a skillet. Griddle cakes (American style pancakes) are pancakes made of a heavier batter.

Pancake batter is made of water or milk, eggs and flour. The batter is poured in a greased skillet which is tilted so that the batter just covers the bottom. If the batter does not run when the skillet is tilted, more water or milk is required. Pancakes are baked for about 1 minute or until the edges curl. Blintz skins are baked on one side only. Hungarian and French pancakes are baked on both sides. Griddle cakes are baked on both sides, 3 or 4 at a time, on a large skillet.

Pancakes are often served as a breakfast dish or as a dessert, filled and topped with whipped cream, meringue or fruit. Batter-made tortillas and Chinese egg rolls are filled with chopped meats or shrimp and vegetables.

BREAD BAKING TOOLS

KNEADING   Two strong hands. A solid wood or formica surface, just a bit lower than hip height. A butcher block is ideal.

MIXING   Wooden paddles, long handled spoons, forks, chopsticks, scoops. Egg beater. Assorted lightweight bowls and measuring cups.

BAKING   Baking pans, casseroles, cookie sheets, muffin tins. Clay baking dishes are good for uniform distribution of heat. In old fashioned ovens bread was baked directly on a tile floor.

SPECIAL EQUIPMENT   For some recipes like Chinese man-t'ou a steamer is called for. Electric beaters, blenders, mixers are helpful when arms tire.

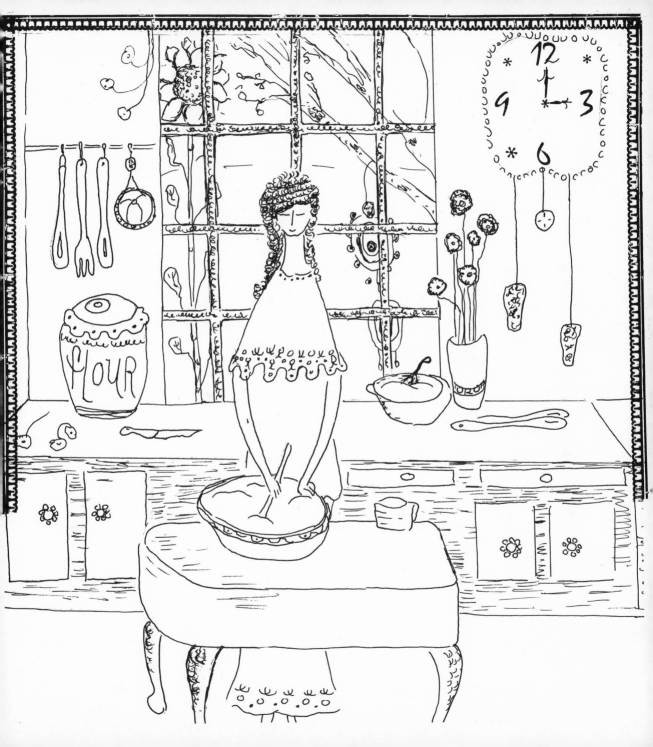

Yeasted

Breads

Ingredients	*1 package dry yeast* *¼ cup warm water* *2 cups milk, scalded* *2 tablespoons honey* *2 teaspoons salt* *1 tablespoon shortening* *6 cups unbleached white flour*
LEAVENING	Soften dry yeast in warm water (110°).
BATTER	Combine hot milk, honey, salt and shortening, and cool to lukewarm. Stir in the yeast mix and 2 cups of flour. Beat well.
DOUGH	Beat in all but 1 cup of the remaining flour to make a moderately stiff dough.
KNEADING	Turn the dough out on a lightly floured surface and knead in the last cup of flour till smooth and satiny (8 to 10 minutes). Knead by pressing down dough with heel of hand, folding back to center, turning and repeating.
RISING	Form dough into a ball and place in a lightly greased bowl, turning once to grease surface. Cover with waxed paper and a towel and let rise in a warm place till double in size (1½ hours). Punch the dough down.
SHAPING	Cut dough in 2 portions and shape into loaves. Place in greased loaf pans. Cover and let rise till double (40 minutes).
BAKING	Bake in hot oven (400°) for 35 minutes or until crusts are golden brown. If tops brown too fast, cover loosely with foil for the last 15 minutes.

Substitute 2 packages of yeast for 1 in white bread recipe, and add 1 beaten egg into the dissolved yeast. Follow white bread recipe until *SHAPING*, then shape rolls into crescents, muffins or cloverleaves as below. After rolls are shaped, let rise 45 minutes (the dough will already have had one rising). Brush tops with melted butter before baking. Bake for 15 minutes in 425° oven or until lightly browned.

CRESCENTS Divide the dough in half and roll out each half to a circle ½" thick. Cut each circle into 12 pie shaped wedges and roll each wedge from the wide side to the point. Place on a greased baking sheet with point side under, and curve each roll to crescent shape.

MUFFINS Divide dough into 24 balls and place each ball in a greased muffin cup.

CLOVER-
LEAVES Divide dough into 72 small balls and place 3 balls side by side in a greased muffin cup. The balls will join to form a cloverleaf in the rising.

BUTTERMILK ROLLS

Substitute 2 packages of yeast for 1 in white bread recipe, and 2 cups of buttermilk for the regular milk. Add ½ teaspoon baking soda and 1 beaten egg to dissolved yeast, and proceed with the white bread recipe to *SHAPING*. Shape into crescents, muffins or cloverleaves as for soft rolls. After rolls are shaped, let rise 45 minutes. Brush tops with melted butter and bake for 15 minutes in 425° oven or until lightly browned.

OATMEAL BREAD

Ingredients	*2 packages dry yeast* *½ cup lukewarm water* *1 cup rolled oats* *1 cup boiling water* *1 cup scalded milk* *2 teaspoons salt* *1 tablespoon vegetable oil* *½ cup molasses or honey* *6½ cups unbleached white flour*

LEAVENING   Dissolve yeast in lukewarm water and let stand for 5 minutes.

BATTER   Pour hot water over rolled oats and cool to lukewarm. Mix the dissolved yeast with milk, salt, oil, and molasses or honey (molasses will yield darker, more pungent bread). Stir in and beat vigorously, 1 cup at a time, 2 cups of flour. Let the batter rest for 5 minutes.

DOUGH   Add, 1 cup at a time, 4 cups of flour, stirring and mixing vigorously after each cup, until difficult to mix. Invert bowl and let dough fall onto lightly floured surface.

KNEADING   Knead in the last ½ cup of flour. The kneading cycle: push down on the ball of dough with the heels of the hands so that it flattens out some-what; fold the edges of the dough back to the center; give the dough a ¼-hour clockwise turn. Find your own rhythm for the knead cycle and knead for about 10 minutes until the dough feels smooth and elastic. If the dough sticks to the hands, add a little more flour.

RISING   Clean a large mixing bowl and rub oil over the bottom half. Form the dough into a ball and place it in the bowl, turning once so that the oiled surface is on top. Cover the bowl with a sheet of waxed paper and a towel and let the dough rise in a warm place away from drafts. It will become about twice its size in 1½ hours. (Oatmeal dough will rise in ordinary room temperature). After rising, poke holes in the dough with a knife, and punch down with your fist. The dough will not recede to its original size entirely.

SHAPING   Divide the dough into 2 parts. Shape each one into a greased bread pan, keeping as flat as possible. Cover with a towel, and this time allow to rise for about 40 minutes in a warm place.

BAKING   Put the shaped dough into the middle of a preheated oven at 325°, and bake for about 45 minutes. After baking, while the bread is still hot, brush melted butter over the crust for shine or added taste.

SERVING   Remove bread from pan and allow to cool on a rack (the broiler rack is fine). Serve plain or with butter.

OATMEAL BREAD VARIATIONS

The basic recipe for oatmeal bread can be varied in many ways and each time it is a new and tasty experience, so try some of these for variety.

OATMEAL WHEAT   For this substitute 3 cups of wheat flour for 3 cups of the unbleached white flour and continue with the remainder of the recipe,
or
Use 2 cups of wheat flour and ½ cup of wheat germ in place of 2½ cups of white flour.

CRACKED WHEAT   An excellent substitute for rolled oats is 1 cup of cracked wheat which may be purchased in an organic or health food store. Cracked wheat bread is of somewhat rougher texture, but has a wonderful taste. In this bread use honey instead of molasses, and 3 cups of wheat flour instead of 3 cups of unbleached white flour.

A traditional English teacake bread eaten hot and buttered, named after Sally Lunn who baked it and hawked it in the streets of Bath.

Ingredients

1 package dry yeast
¼ cup warm water
¾ cup warm milk (110°)
3 tablespoons butter
3 tablespoons sugar
3 eggs
3 cups unbleached white flour
1¼ teaspoons salt

LEAVENING

Soften yeast in warm water. Add milk and set aside for 5 minutes.

BATTER

Cream butter and sugar. Add eggs one at a time, beating after each addition. Combine flour and salt and add to creamed mixture alternatively with yeast mixture, beating well until batter is smooth.

RISING

Cover batter and let rise till double (1 hour). Beat down and pour into well greased 9" tube pan. Let rise again till double (30 minutes).

BAKING

Bake at 350° for 40 minutes.

SERVING

Remove from pan and serve hot with butter.

ANADAMA CHEESE BREAD

Ingredients   2 packages dry yeast
½ cup warm water
1½ cups water
½ cup cornmeal
2 teaspoons salt
¼ cup vegetable shortening
½ cup honey
6 cups unbleached white flour
2 cups shredded cheese
2 tablespoons melted butter or margarine
1 tablespoon cornmeal (for topping)

LEAVENING   Sprinkle yeast into ½ cup warm water. Let stand for 5 minutes.

BATTER   Combine 1½ cups water, ½ cup cornmeal, salt, shortening and molasses in a medium sized saucepan. Heat, stirring constantly, until thick and bubbly. Pour into a large bowl and cool to lukewarm. Stir yeast mix into cornmeal mix. Beat in 2 cups of flour until smooth; stir in cheese, then beat in, one cup at a time, 3½ cups flour. Invert bowl and let dough fall onto lightly floured board.

KNEADING   Knead in the last ½ cup of flour. If mixture is sticky add a bit more flour. Press down on dough with the heels of the hands, fold dough toward the center and give a ¼-hour clockwise turn. Repeat kneading until dough is smooth and does not stick to the hands.

RISING   Shape dough into a smooth ball and put into a greased bowl. Turn once so top is greased. Cover with wax paper and towel and allow to rise in a warm place 1½ hours or until dough is double in bulk.

SHAPING   Divide dough in half, then divide one half into 15 balls, smoothing each ball with the hands. Place a row of 5 balls along each side of a bread pan with a row of 5 balls in the center. Repeat with remaining half of dough in a second loaf pan. Brush tops of loaves with melted butter and sprinkle lightly with cornmeal. Let rise in a warm place about 30 minutes or until double in bulk.

BAKING   Bake in a moderate oven (375°) for 35 minutes, or until loaves give a hollow sound when tapped. When cooled, loaves will break into rolls for serving.

CHALLAH OR SABBATH BREAD

In some cookbooks recipes for Challah include milk. It would be inconceivable for a Jewish cook, observing the dietary laws, to prepare her Friday night bread with milk, since meat and dairy products are always kept separate.

Ingredients

2 packages dry yeast
1½ cups warm water
4 eggs
¼ cup oil
2 teaspoons salt
¼ cup honey
9½ cups unbleached white flour

LEAVENING

Dissolve yeast in ½ cup warm water. Let stand for 5 minutes.

BATTER

Beat eggs, reserving 1 yolk for use later on the crust, into a large bowl, and add dissolved yeast, oil, honey and 1 cup warm water. Beat in, 2 cups at a time, 6 cups of flour until a smooth batter is formed. Let rest for 5 minutes.

DOUGH

Add in the remaining flour, a little at a time, stirring constantly. When dough no longer sticks to the bowl, turn out onto lightly floured board.

KNEADING

Knead thoroughly. If dough becomes sticky, add a bit more flour. Kneading cycle: push down and away on dough with heels of the hands; give dough a ¼ turn; fold dough back toward center. Continue kneading for 10 minutes or until dough is smooth and elastic. There will be a rather large mass of dough and you may find it easier to divide dough in 2.

RISING

Place dough in a large oiled bowl and turn once to grease top. Cover with waxed paper and a towel and let rise 1½ hours or until doubled in bulk.

SHAPING   Punch dough down and shape on a floured board into the following optional shapes:

BRAIDED   Cut dough into 3 parts and pull each part out to a length of 30'', thicker in the middle and tapered at the ends. Braid the 3 lengths together, starting from one end, and seal ends. Place diagonally on baking tin.

ROUNDED   In a large oiled casserole place most of the large mound of dough, reserving about ¼ of it. Make 4 balls out of the reserved part. Place 3 of the balls on top of the large mound and the 4th ball on top of the 3.

RECTANGLES   Cut dough into 3 parts. Place each part in a separate oiled bread pan. Smooth down the tops by patting.

BAKING   Brush tops with most of the beaten egg yolk, and let rise for 30 minutes. Bake for 15 minutes at 350°, then brush top of Challah again with remaining egg yolk. Bake for 25 more minutes or until a rich brown. Cool on wire rack.

SERVING   Challah is traditionally served on Friday night, the Sabbath night for Jews.

Ingredients	*4 cups unbleached white flour*
	2 packages dry yeast
	3 tablespoons honey
	1 teaspoon salt
	1¼ cups very warm water (110°)

LEAVENING Dissolve yeast in warm water and let stand 5 minutes.

BATTER Mix 2 cups of flour, 2 tablespoons of honey and salt into the dissolved yeast, beating vigorously to produce a smooth batter.

DOUGH Add one more cup of flour to the batter, beating thoroughly. Invert bowl and let dough fall onto a lightly floured board.

KNEADING Knead in the last cup of flour. Continue kneading, pushing dough away with heels of hands, folding edges back to center, then giving dough a ¼ turn, until dough is smooth and moderately stiff.

SHAPING Cut the dough into 12 portions and shape each into a smooth ball. Punch a hole in the center of each ball with floured forefinger. Pull gently to enlarge hole, working each bagel into uniform shape.

RISING Cover with waxed paper and a towel and let rise 25 minutes at room temperature.

BOILING AND BAKING In a large pot bring 1 gallon water and 1 tablespoon of honey to boil. Reduce to simmering and cook bagels 4 or 5 at a time for 7 minutes, turning once. Drain on absorbent towels. Place on a greased baking sheet and bake at 375° for 30 minutes or until golden brown.

SERVING Traditionally served with cream cheese and lox. Good too with just butter.

ONION Sauté ½ cup finely chopped onions in 3 tablespoons butter, till tender but not brown. Brush onion-butter mix over tops of bagels after first 20 minutes of baking.

WHOLE
WHEAT The method is the same for whole wheat bagels as for regular bagels, but with the following ingredients substituted for the regular ones.

Ingredients
2½ cups unbleached white flour
2 packages dry yeast
1½ cups very warm water (110°)
2 tablespoons honey
1 teaspoon salt
1½ cups whole wheat flour

Ingredients   *1 package dry yeast*
1¼ cups warm water
2 tablespoons melted butter
1 teaspoon salt
4 cups unbleached white flour
Egg white mixed with 1 teaspoon water

LEAVENING   Stir yeast into warm water and let stand 5 minutes.

BATTER   Add melted butter, salt and 2 cups of flour to the dissolved yeast and beat thoroughly until smooth.

DOUGH   Beat in 1½ more cups of flour to form a dough. Invert bowl and let dough fall on lightly floured surface.

KNEADING   Knead in last ½ cup of flour by pressing down on dough with the heels of the hands, giving a ¼ turn, and folding dough back toward center. Knead till dough is smooth and elastic, about 10 minutes.

RISING   Place ball of dough in a greased bowl, turning once to grease top. Cover with waxed paper and towel and let rise in a warm place until doubled in bulk, about 1½ hours. Punch dough down with fist, cover and let rise again for 45 minutes.

SHAPING   Punch dough down and turn onto lightly floured surface. Roll dough into a 14"x 10" rectangle. Roll the rectangle into a long scroll and pinch the ends to seal. Gently roll the scroll, pulling to shape and taper into a long thin loaf.

Place the loaf diagonally on a greased cookie sheet. Make 6 shallow, diagonal cuts on top and brush with egg mix. Cover so towel does not touch dough and let rise 40 minutes.

BAKING   Brush again with egg mix and bake for 10 minutes at 400°. Brush again with egg mix. Lower heat to 375° and bake for 30 minutes or until golden brown.

For crustiness place a shallow pan filled with boiling water under the bread while baking.

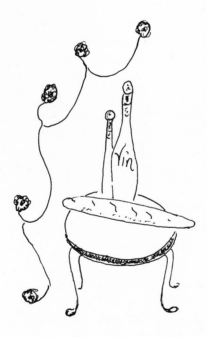

CUBAN BREAD

Ingredients	*1 package dry yeast* *2 cups very warm water (110°)* *2 teaspoons salt* *6 cups unbleached white flour* *ice water*
LEAVENING	Dissolve yeast in very warm water in a large bowl.
BATTER	Beat 2 cups of flour into leavening until smooth.
DOUGH	Beat in 3½ cups of the remaining flour to make a soft dough.
KNEADING	Turn dough out onto a lightly floured board. Knead in the last ½ cup flour. Continue kneading, pushing dough down and away with heels of the hands, then folding dough back toward the center and giving it a ¼ turn clockwise. Keep kneading until dough is smooth and elastic, about 10 minutes, using only as much flour as needed to prevent sticking.
RISING	Place in a greased large bowl and turn to coat all over with oil. Cover with waxed paper and towel. Let rise in warm place 1½ hours or until double in bulk.
SHAPING	Punch the dough down, turn out onto a board, and let rest for 10 minutes. Divide dough in half and knead each piece a few times. Roll out one piece to a 15"x 10" rectangle. Roll up tightly from long side, jelly-roll fashion and pinch long seam to seal. Roll loaf gently back and forth to taper ends. Place loaf diagonally on a large cookie sheet which has been greased and sprinkled with cornmeal.
	Pat out second piece of dough to an 8" round and place on a greased and cornmealed cookie sheet. Let both loaves rise again in a warm place 45 minutes. Make slits 2" apart on tops with a sharp knife.

BAKING   Brush loaves with ice water and place cookie sheets in cold oven. Turn
oven to hot (400°) and bake 45 minutes, brushing several times with ice
water. Cool on wire rack.

RUSSIAN BLACK BREAD

Ingrédients

2 packages dry yeast
½ cup warm water
4 cups rye flour
2 teaspoons salt
2 cups whole bran cereal
2 tablespoons caraway seeds, crushed
2 teaspoons postum or instant coffee
½ teaspoon fennel seeds, crushed
2½ cups water
¼ cup vinegar
¼ cup molasses
1 tablespoon honey
¼ cup oil
2 cups unbleached white flour
1 cup graham flour
1 teaspoon cornstarch

LEAVENING

Mix yeast in ½ cup warm water and let stand for 5 minutes.

BATTER

Mix 3 of the 4 cups of rye flour with salt, bran, postum or coffee, fennel and caraway. Pour 2 cups of water, vinegar, molasses, honey and oil in a saucepan and heat to lukewarm. Stir the liquid mixture into the dry mixture, add the dissolved yeast and beat together to make a smooth batter. Allow the batter to rest for 5 minutes.

DOUGH

Add the last cup of rye flour and the white flour to the batter, beating vigorously. Turn the dough onto a lightly floured board and work in the graham flour to make a smooth but fairly stiff dough.

KNEADING

Knead thoroughly: press dough down with heels of hands, pushing dough away; fold dough back toward you, giving a ¼ turn. Continue kneading for 10 minutes or until dough feels smooth and elastic.

RISING   Place dough in a clean greased bowl, turning to grease top. Cover and put in a warm place to rise until doubled in bulk, about 1½ hours.

SHAPING   Punch dough down. Divide into 2, shape each half into a ball, and place each ball in a greased 8'' pan. Cover and let rise again in a warm place about 40 minutes.

BAKING   Preheat oven to 350° and bake 45 minutes or until bread sounds hollow to the tap. Meanwhile combine cornstarch and ½ cup water in a saucepan. Heat, stirring until mixture thickens, about 2 minutes. Brush hot mixture over baked breads. Return breads to the oven and bake 2 more minutes or until glaze is set. Cool on a rack.

SERVING   This bread improves with age. Let cool completely before slicing. Thin slices are best. Wrapped well, the black bread will be excellent for many days.

Ingredients

1 package active dry yeast
1¾ cups warm water
¼ cup honey
¼ cup molasses
1 tablespoon salt
2 tablespoons oil
2 cups rye flour
3 tablespoons caraway seed
4 to 4½ cups unbleached white flour

LEAVENING   Dissolve yeast in ¼ cup warm water and let stand for 5 minutes.

BATTER   In large bowl, stir honey, molasses, salt and shortening with 1½ cups warm water. Add yeast, caraway seeds and rye flour. Beat in vigorously 2 cups of white flour and let batter rest for 5 minutes.

DOUGH   Beat into batter, 2 more cups of white flour. Invert bowl and allow the dough to fall on lightly floured board.

KNEADING   Knead in the last ½ cup of white flour, by pushing down on the dough with heels of the hands, and folding dough back toward center with a ¼ turn. Knead for 10 minutes or until dough is smooth and satiny.

RISING   Place dough in lightly greased bowl, turning once to grease surface. Cover with waxed paper and a towel and let rise in a warm place until double in bulk (1½ hours).

SHAPING   Pat dough into 2 round loaves and place each on an 8'' greased round cake pan. Cover and let rise until double (about 40 minutes).

BAKING   Bake at 375° for about 25 minutes. For soft glistening crust, brush with melted butter and put back in oven for 5 more minutes.

Ingredients	*1 package dry yeast*
	½ cup warm water (110°)
	¾ cup warm milk
	2 cups rye flour
	2 cups unbleached white flour
	¼ cup butter
	2 tablespoons honey
	Pinch salt
	¼ cup molasses
	1 teaspoon orange juice

LEAVENING   Dissolve yeast in warm water and let stand for 5 minutes.

BATTER   Melt butter in warm milk. Add molasses, honey, salt, yeast and orange juice. Beat white flour thoroughly into this mixture until smooth.

DOUGH   Beat in rye flour a cup at a time, reserving ½ cup for kneading.

KNEADING   Let dough drop onto lightly floured board. Knead in last ½ cup of flour by pushing down with the heels of the hands, giving dough ¼ turn and folding dough over toward center. Knead for 10 minutes or until dough is smooth and firm.

SHAPING   Divide dough in 3 parts and roll out in long loaves. Place on oiled cookie sheets.

RISING   Let rise in a warm place until doubled, 1½ hours.

BAKING   Bake in 375° oven for 20 minutes. When loaves are completely cool, slice them in half lengthwise, then into 1'' slices. Place on baking sheets and dry in slow oven (300°) until light brown. Turn off heat and leave rusks until thoroughly dry and crisp.

ROUND ITALIAN BREAD

Ingredients
2 packages dry yeast
2½ cups warm water (110°)
1 tablespoon salt
7½ cups unbleached white flour
Yellow corn meal
Egg mix (1 slightly beaten egg and 1 tablespoon water)

LEAVENING
Stir yeast into warm water and let stand 5 minutes.

BATTER
In a large bowl, beat 2 cups of flour together with the yeast mix, adding salt, to make a smooth batter.

DOUGH
Beat in 4½ cups of the remaining flour. The dough will be stiff. Turn out onto a lightly floured board, and knead in remaining flour.

KNEADING
Knead about 10 minutes by pressing down with heels of hands, folding dough, giving ¼ turn and so on until dough is smooth and elastic.

RISING
Form dough into ball, place in a lightly greased bowl, and turn once to grease surface. Cover and let rise till doubled (1½ hours). Punch dough down and form ball again. Let rise once more till doubled (1 hour). Turn out on lightly floured surface and divide into 2 balls.

SHAPING
Flatten the two balls slightly and place on greased baking sheets sprinkled with corn meal (this gives a crunchy bottom crust). With a sharp knife make 4 shallow cuts, 1'' apart, across top, then 4 crosswise cuts. Brush egg mix over tops and sides of loaves. Cover with a damp tent made by placing cloth over tall tumblers. Let rise ½ an hour.
sprinkle on sesame seeds

BAKING
For crispy crust place pan of boiling water on lower rack of oven. Bake at 375° for 20 minutes. Brush again with egg mix and bake another 20 minutes or until nicely browned. Makes 2 loaves.

ITALIAN ROLLS

Follow recipe for round Italian bread up to *SHAPING*. At that point form the dough into 18 balls or 18 ovals tapered at each end. Make 2 shallow cuts diagonally across each top. Place rolls on a greased cookie sheet and bake 20 minutes in a 400° oven, or until golden brown.

ITALIAN BREAD STICKS

Follow recipe for round Italian bread up to *SHAPING*. At that point divide dough into 28 balls. Gently roll each ball between the fingers to a pencil about 8'' long. Lay sticks out on a greased cookie sheet and brush with egg mix. Coarse salt or minced garlic may be sprinkled on top if desired. Bake bread sticks in preheated 425° oven for 10 minutes or until golden brown.

If the man in the house likes to have his day in the kitchen here's a recipe he'll find irresistible, both in making and eating. So clear the decks and stay out of his way. This one requires a lot of beating and pounding and a strong arm on the rolling pin.

Ingredients

1 tablespoon vegetable oil
½ package dry yeast
2½ to 3 cups unbleached white flour
1 cup whole wheat flour
or
½ cup whole wheat and ½ cup soybean flour
1 tablespoon dry milk
¾ cup warm water

LEAVENING

Mix yeast in ¼ cup warm water and allow to stand for 5 minutes.

BATTER

Mix oil and dry milk in ½ cup warm water, then gradually add white flour and whole wheat or whole wheat and soybean mixture, beating actively until the whole is of creamy consistency. Soybean makes for a more nutritious pizza.

DOUGH

Add the yeast mixture to the batter, stirring it in thoroughly with as much additional flour as is necessary to produce a ball of dough that does not stick to the fingers, but which is still quite malleable.

KNEADING

Sprinkle flour lightly on work surface, and begin kneading the ball of of dough by pushing it away with the heel of the hand and folding the edges back repeatedly. If the dough begins to feel moist again, sprinkle more flour on the work surface. Continue kneading for about 8 minutes or until the dough is malleable but firm.

RISING

Form the dough into a ball and place it in a bowl with a little vegetable oil in the bottom. Turn the ball over, thus greasing it slightly. Cover the bowl with wax paper and a towel, and let rise in a warm oven (80°) for about 1½ hours. Punch the dough down, and form again into a ball. Cover with wax paper and towel and let rise again for around 45 minutes.

SHAPING

Punch the dough down, fold the edges over, and cut enough off to form a ball slightly larger than a baseball. This is enough for a sizable pizza crust. The remaining dough may be used for a second, smaller pizza or may be shaped into several assorted rolls.

Sprinkle flour on a large (14''x 17'') cookie sheet, which should be without edges at least on two sides so that a rolling pin can be used on it. Shake the cookie sheet vigorously until the flour powders uniformly over it. This will keep the dough from sticking to the sheet. Flatten the dough between the palms, and holding thus between the palms at one end, allow the dough to stretch down a little by gravity. Keep clasping the dough between the palms at different places, allowing the dough to stretch more and more. This is the cautious substitute for tossing the dough in the air.

Place the flattened and stretched dough on the cookie sheet, and roll out in every direction with a rolling pin, until the sheet is completely and evenly covered with a thin dough. Dough that protrudes over the edges of the sheet may be cut off and plugged back in where needed to fill excessively thin places. When the whole sheet is covered, raise the edges of the dough slightly by drawing them up between the heels of the cupped hands. The pizza crust is now ready to receive topping.

PIZZA
TOPPING

While the pizza crust is being made, the sauce for the topping should be bubbling on the stove.

> 2 cans tomato paste
> 2 cans water (use tomato paste can)
> ¾ lb Italian sausage
> ¾ teaspoon oregano
> 1 teaspoon sweet basil
> salt and pepper to taste
> Mozzarella cheese
> grated Parmesan cheese
> green pepper, sliced thin
> thin rings of raw onion

Cook sausage in water for about 10 minutes or until pink color is gone. Remove sausage and slice thin. Put slices on heavy skillet and brown for a few minutes. Meanwhile combine tomato paste, water, oregano, sweet basil, salt and pepper, and cook over low heat for 40 minutes.

BAKING

With a spoon spread tomato sauce over the entire surface of the pizza. Sprinkle the surface lightly with oil. Bake at 425° for 10 minutes. Remove from oven and cover with sliced sausage, thin slices or shreds of Mozzarella, green pepper, and onion rings. Cover all with grated Parmesan. Bake for 8 more minutes in 400° oven or until Mozzarella has melted.

SERVING

If the second pizza is to be frozen, do not put on the Mozzarella, green peppers, onions or sausages until ready to serve. Freeze the pizza with just tomato sauce; all else should be put on fresh.

When the pizza comes out of the oven, cut into squares with a serrated knife and serve piping hot. A large pizza serves 2 big eaters.

Ingredients	*2 packages dry yeast*
	2¼ cups warm water
	¾ cup milk
	1 tablespoon honey
	2 teaspoons salt
	3 tablespoons vegetable oil
	6½ cups unbleached white flour, sifted
	¼ cup toasted sesame seeds
	1 egg, beaten

LEAVENING Dissolve yeast in warm water and let stand 5 minutes.

BATTER Mix milk, honey, salt and oil in large bowl and add the dissolved yeast. Beat in 2 cups of flour to make a smooth batter.

DOUGH Beat in enough of the remaining flour to make a soft dough, then turn out onto a lightly floured board.

KNEADING Knead until smooth and elastic, about 10 minutes, by pressing down on dough with heels of the hands, folding back dough, giving a ¼ turn and repeating. Add only as much flour as need to keep dough from sticking.

RISING Form dough into ball, place in greased bowl, turning once to grease top. Cover with waxed paper and towel and place in warm place to rise (1½ hours).

SHAPING Punch dough down and divide into 4 pieces. Divide 1 of these pieces into 3. Grease 3 cookie sheets. Pat out 1 of the large pieces of dough to a 9'' round on a cookie sheet. Make a 3'' hole in the center of the round by pulling dough back with fingers. Make a 3'' round of one of the small pieces of dough and place it in center. Repeat to make 3 loaves. Cover lightly and set aside to rise for 40 minutes.

BAKING   Brush breads with beaten egg and sprinkle with sesame seeds. Bake at 350° for 30 minutes or until breads give a hollow sound when tapped. Remove from cookie sheets to wire racks to cool.

This Persian bread (nan) is traditionally baked on a floor of pebbles (sangak).

Ingredients	*2 cups warm water*
	1 package dry yeast
	5 cups whole wheat flour

LEAVENING   Dissolve yeast in warm water and let stand for 5 minutes.

BATTER   Pour the dissolved yeast into 2½ cups of flour and beat vigorously till the batter is smooth.

DOUGH   Reserve ½ cup flour for kneading, and beat in the remainder to obtain a soft dough.

KNEADING   Let dough fall onto lightly floured surface. Knead in the remaining ½ cup of flour by pressing down on the dough with the heels of the hands, folding back toward center, and giving ¼ turn. Knead for 10 minutes or until dough is smooth. If dough sticks add a bit more flour.

RISING   Place ball of dough in lightly oiled bowl and turn once to oil top. Cover with waxed paper and cloth and let rise in a warm place for 1½ hours or until doubled in bulk.

SHAPING   Divide dough into 6 parts and form each into a ball. With floured hands flatten each ball and shape into a circle ½'' thick.

BAKING   Bake on ungreased cookie sheet 3 at a time at 475° for 5 minutes or until lightly browned. For authentic Persian method, cover bottom of a large pan with washed, smooth beach pebbles. Heat pan in oven for 5 minutes at 450°, then place 2 breads at a time on the pebbles and bake for 5 minutes.

SYRIAN BREAD

Ingredients
    2 packages dry yeast
    ½ cup very warm water (110°)
    5½ cups unbleached white flour
    1½ cups milk
    3 tablespoons honey
    3 tablespoons oil
    2 teaspoons salt

LEAVENING   Dissolve yeast in warm water and let stand for 5 minutes.

BATTER   Warm milk, honey, oil and salt on stove, stirring constantly. Pour into large bowl with yeast mixture, and beat in 3 cups of flour until smooth.

DOUGH   Beat in thoroughly 2 more cups of flour to form a moderately stiff dough.

KNEADING   Knead in the last ½ cup of flour by pushing down on the dough with the heels of the hands, folding dough back toward you, giving the dough a ¼ turn, and repeating. Knead for 10 minutes or until dough is smooth and elastic. If dough sticks, sprinkle flour on board while kneading.

RISING   Place dough in a greased bowl and turn once to grease top. Cover and let rise till doubled (1½ hours). Punch down and let rest 10 minutes.

SHAPING   Shape into balls 1½'' in diameter. Place the balls on an ungreased baking sheet and roll each into a 4'' circle.

BAKING   Bake at 400° for 8 minutes or until puffed. Cool on a cloth covered surface. Makes 30 flat breads.

Ingredients	*1 package dry yeast*
	1 cup warm water (110°)
	1 teaspoon honey
	2 cups unbleached white flour
	1¾ cups whole wheat flour
	1 teaspoon salt
	Corn meal

LEAVENING Stir yeast into water and let stand 5 minutes.

BATTER Beat dissolved yeast thoroughly into 2 cups of white flour until batter is smooth.

DOUGH Continue beating the whole wheat flour and salt into the batter until a dough is formed. Let dough fall onto corn meal sprinkled surface.

KNEADING With corn meal on hands, knead dough about 10 minutes by pressing down with heels of the hands, folding dough, giving a ¼ turn. Repeat until dough is smooth and elastic.

SHAPING Divide dough into 12 balls. Roll each ball into a very thin circle 6½'' in diameter on a corn meal dusted surface.

RISING Cover with a towel and let rise for 35 minutes. Roll thin again and let rise for 30 minutes.

BAKING Have 3 large cookie sheets ready. Place 4 breads on each ungreased cookie sheet and bake quickly, about 4 minutes in 475° oven, or until breads are puffed out and just a bit brown.

SERVING Serve warm.

The Chinese prepare bread by steaming or frying on top of the stove. Bread is not a staple Chinese food, but is regional to northern China.

Ingredients

3¼ cups unbleached white flour
1¼ cups warm water
1 package dry yeast

LEAVENING   Dissolve yeast in water in a bowl and let stand for 5 minutes.

DOUGH   Add flour slowly to the yeast mixture, stirring and beating vigorously until dough is formed and until it does not stick to the bowl.

KNEADING   Turn the dough out onto a lightly floured surface and knead for about 4 minutes. Knead by pushing down and away with the heels of the hands, folding dough back, giving dough a ¼ turn, and so on.

RISING   Form dough into a ball and place in a greased bowl. Turn once to grease top. Cover with waxed paper and towel and let rise 1½ hours in a warm place.

SHAPING   Punch dough down and shape into 12 balls about 2" in diameter. Place the balls on a piece of cheesecloth cut to fit your steamer tier. Allow 2" of space around each ball for expansion. Let rest for 10 minutes.

STEAMING   Steam over boiling water for 20 minutes.

SERVING   Remove from the steamer and serve warm with meat or vegetable dish.

Pao-tzŭ are filled man-t'ou. A shrimp filling is shown below. Try other fillings as well, such as sweet and sour pork sliced very thin. An all vegetable mix can be used, with Chinese cabbage, onions, broccoli, sliced thin and diced small, and quickly stir-fried in oil with soy sauce. Left over chicken is excellent in place of shrimp.

Ingredients

3¼ cups unbleached white flour
1¼ cups warm water
1 package dry yeast
Filling:
1 cup celery
2 scallions
¼ cup small shrimp
1 tablespoon soy sauce
Minced garlic to taste

FILLING

With a sharp paring knife cut celery and scallions into very thin slices on the bias. Mix shrimp, soy sauce, garlic and vegetables, and quickly stir-fry in a small quantity of oil on a hot iron griddle or in a Chinese wock, stirring constantly with a wooden spoon. If griddle gets too hot, turn heat down or lift griddle from stove occasionally. Total time for frying should be about 3 minutes.

SHAPING

Prepare man-t'ou according to recipe up to shaping. Shape into balls as directed and then make a hollow in each ball by pressing in with the fingers. Place a tablespoon of filling in each hollow and pull the dough over to enclose the filling. Turn pao-tzŭ so smooth side is on top and place on steaming tier, 2'' apart. Let rest 10 minutes.

STEAMING

Steam over boiling water for 20 minutes.

SERVING

Remove from steamer and serve warm.

Sourdough

Breads

Here is a recipe for a starter that takes 48 hours to ferment. You don't have to sit around and watch it, though. Just prepare and let it work for you while you are off shopping or getting a good night's sleep.

Ingredients

5 medium potatoes peeled and quartered
½ cup unbleached white flour
2 quarts boiling water
1 package dry yeast
½ cup lukewarm water
¼ cup honey
2 tablespoons salt

Stir yeast into lukewarm water and let stand for 5 minutes.

Cook potatoes in boiling water until very tender. Mash potatoes or put in a blender to puree, then mix with potato water in its entirety. Cool to lukewarm and add yeast mix, honey and flour, stirring till creamy.

Remove to a large, clean bowl, cover, and put in a warm place to ferment for 48 hours. You're now ready to make your sourdough bread. If you wish to store the starter for future use, refrigerate in a covered jar.

SOURDOUGH FRENCH BREAD

Ingredients	*1 package dry yeast*
	1 cup starter
	1 cup lukewarm water
	1 tablespoon oil
	1 teaspoon salt
	5 cups unbleached white flour

LEAVENING

Mix yeast into lukewarm water with starter and let stand 5 minutes, then stir until completely blended.

DOUGH

Add flour 1 cup at a time, blending well after each addition. Turn on to lightly floured board and fold a few times until dough feels smooth. If dough is sticky add more flour.

RISING

Form dough in a ball and place in a greased bowl, turning once to grease top. Cover with waxed paper and a towel. Let rise in a warm place until doubled (1½ hours).

KNEADING

Punch the dough a little, knead it slightly, and hit it against the board just enough to remove the bubbles.

SHAPING

With a rolling pin, roll the dough into an oblong ½'' thick. Then, jelly-roll fashion, roll it together, sealing the edges. Place dough on a greased cookie sheet sprinkled with corn meal. Gently pull and stretch into a long tapered shape.

BAKING

Bake in a preheated 450° oven for 15 minutes. Lower the temperature to 375° and bake for 20 minutes more or until bread is golden brown. Remove from oven to cool. For crispy crust keep a pan of boiling water on bottom shelf of oven.

SERVING

Slice at an angle and warm in foil before serving.

This crusty rye can be made with potato sourdough starter. Your starter turns into sponge I, then sponge II, and finally into dough - a slow development where most of the action takes place without the baker.

Ingredients	*2 cups sourdough starter*
	1 package dry yeast
	2½ cups warm water
	6 cups rye flour
	1 tablespoon salt
	1 tablespoon caraway seeds
	2 cups unbleached white flour
	Egg water (1 egg and 1 tablespoon water)

SPONGE I

Take 2 cups sourdough starter, mix in 2 cups rye flour and ½ cup water. Cover with towel and put aside for 3 hours. Mixture will get bubbly and will rise and fall.

SPONGE II

Mix 1 package dry yeast, 1 cup warm water, and 3 cups rye flour. Add this mixture to sponge I. Mix all to a smooth consistency. Cover and let rise for 2 hours.

DOUGH

Mix salt, 1 cup warm water, caraway seeds, 2 cups white flour, and 1 cup rye flour. Stir this mixture together with sponge II so that the two blend, but don't overmix or knead. If dough is sticky add a bit more flour. Let stand for 5 minutes.

SHAPING

Mold into 2 or 3 round shapes or long loaves and place on corn meal sprinkled sheets. Proof, that is, let rise for 15 minutes in an oven with a pan of boiling water on the bottom shelf, or in any warm, moist place.

BAKING   Deflate dough a little with a few pokes of a sharp knife. Bake for 50 minutes in a 375° oven with a pan of boiling water on the bottom shelf. Renew the water from time to time.

To put an extra shine on the crust, brush an egg water mixture over the top of the bread before putting into oven, and again half way through the baking.

SERVING   Cool on a wire rack. Serve with butter or slice thin for delicious sandwiches of kosher delicatessen, cheese, or egg salad. Whatever goes inside can only be improved by the taste of this bread.

Ingredients	*2 packages dry yeast*
	2½ cups warm water
	5 cups rye flour
	¾ cup unbleached white flour
	½ cup wheat germ
	½ cup bran
	½ cup graham flour
	1 tablespoon caraway seeds

SOUR DOUGH STARTER   Dissolve 1 package yeast in ½ cup warm water. Mix in 1 cup rye flour, cover with towel and let stand overnight in a warm place.

SPONGE I   To the starter add another cup of warm water with 1 more cup of rye flour. Let ferment 3½ hours.

SPONGE II   Dissolve 1 package yeast in 1 cup of warm water. Add 3 cups rye flour and mix into Sponge I. Ferment for 3 hours.

DOUGH   To Sponge II add wheat germ, bran, graham, white flour and caraway seeds. Mix until the dough is smooth.

RISING   Cover with towel and let rise in warm place for 45 minutes.

KNEADING   Knead on floured surface by pushing, turning and folding, until dough is smooth and elastic, about 10 minutes.

SHAPING   Shape into 3 round loaves and place each on a greased baking sheet sprinkled with corn meal. Cover and let rise for 30 minutes.

BAKING   With a pan of boiling water beneath the bread for the first hour, bake at 425° for ½ hour and 350° for 1 hour.

SOURDOUGH PANCAKES

Ingredients
1 cup starter (see p. 59)
1 teaspoon baking soda
½ teaspoon salt
1 egg, well beaten
2 tablespoons oil
1 tablespoon maple syrup
½ cup unbleached white flour

BATTER
Stir all dry ingredients together in a large bowl. Mix all liquid ingredients into the starter and add all at once to the dry mix, stirring well. Milk or water may be added if batter is too thick to pour.

BAKING
Bake on a hot griddle, turning with spatula to brown both sides.

SERVING
Serve hot with any kind of maple or fruit syrup, or with fresh berries. Makes about 12 medium sized pancakes.

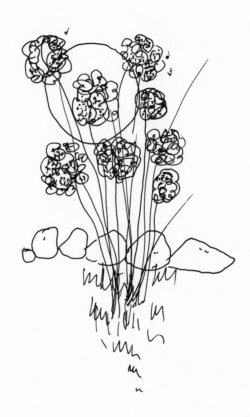

Yeasted

Sweet

Breads

This basic sweet dough can, with minor modifications, be made into cinnamon rolls, holiday bread or coffee cake. The recipe given is for sweet rolls, and variations follow.

Ingredients

1 package dry yeast
¼ cup warm water
3½ cups unbleached white flour
¾ cup milk
¼ cup honey
2 tablespoons vegetable oil
1 teaspoon salt
2 eggs

LEAVENING

Dissolve yeast in warm water and let stand for 5 minutes.

BATTER

Heat milk, honey, oil and salt until just warm. Thoroughly beat in 2 cups of flour. Then stir in the dissolved yeast and eggs and beat together until batter is smooth.

DOUGH

Beat in one more cup of flour until a dough is formed which does not stick to the bowl.

KNEADING

Invert bowl and let dough fall on lightly floured board. Knead in the last ½ cup of flour by pushing down on dough with the heels of the hands, giving dough a ¼ turn and folding dough toward center. Knead until dough is smooth and pliable, about 8 minutes.

RISING

Shape dough into a ball and place in oiled bowl. Turn once to oil top. Cover with waxed paper and a towel and let rise in a warm place till doubled, about 1½ hours.

SHAPING   Punch dough down and divide it in half. Roll out each half into a rectangle, then roll up each rectangle jelly-roll fashion, making sure uneven edge remains on the bottom. Slice each roll into 12 portions and place cut side down on greased cookie sheet. Cover and let rise about 40 minutes.

BAKING   Bake at 375° for 20 minutes or until golden brown.

SWEET DOUGH VARIATIONS

CINNAMON ROLLS   Before dough is rolled into jelly-roll, spread a mixture of ¼ cup sugar, 1 tablespoon cinnamon and ¼ cup melted butter, then roll and continue.

HOLIDAY BREAD   Fold ½ cup of chopped nuts and ½ cup of glazed fruits into the batter, and also add 1 teaspoon of almond extract. Roll the dough out into a *single* rectangle instead of 2, and roll up jelly-roll fashion into a loaf. Bake in a greased bread pan at 350° for 45 minutes.

COFFEE CAKE   Follow cinnamon roll variation, adding ½ cup chopped walnuts before rolling into jelly-rolls. Shape each jelly-roll into a half moon, pinching ends to taper. Brush an egg wash made of 1 egg yolk, 1 tablespoon of brown sugar and 1 tablespoon of milk, on the tops of the half moons. Sprinkle a handful of walnut slivers over egg wash and set cakes aside to rise for 40 minutes. Continue with basic sweet dough recipe.

If you have plenty of time and like gourmet food, here's a delicious
French treat for breakfast.

Ingredients
1 package dry yeast
¼ cup warm water
½ cup milk
½ lb softened butter
¼ cup sugar
½ teaspoon salt
4 cups unbleached white flour, sifted
3 eggs
1 egg yolk
1 tablespoon milk

LEAVENING   Soften yeast in warm water and let stand for 5 minutes.

BATTER   Scald milk and pour over butter, sugar and salt in a bowl. Allow to stand
             until lukewarm. Mix in thoroughly ½ cup sifted flour. Stir the yeast mix-
             ture into this, then beat in, with a large spoon, 1½ cups sifted flour.
             Add the 3 eggs, one at a time, beating well after each.

DOUGH   Add in, one cup at a time, the last 2 cups of sifted flour. Beat thorough-
             ly for 8 minutes or until a soft smooth dough is formed. Brush top with
             melted butter.

RISING   Cover the dough with waxed paper and a towel. Set in a warm place
             (80°) to rise. When doubled (1½ hours), punch down. Butter surface and
             cover again. Set in refrigerator for 12 hours or overnight. Punch dough
             down once or twice as it rises.

SHAPING   Remove dough from refrigerator and place it on a lightly floured surface.
             Shape 2/3 of the dough into 2'' balls and place them in buttered 3''

muffin cups. Form an equal number of small balls from the remaining 1/3 of dough. Gently roll each ball to cone shape between palms of the hands. With index finger make an impression in center of larger balls. Insert tips of cones in the impressions. These cone-shaped pieces of dough form the "top hats". Cover loosely with towel and set in warm place until doubled (½ hour).

BAKING   Brush lightly with a mix of 1 egg yolk and a tablespoon of milk, and bake at 425° for 15 minutes or until nicely browned.

SERVING   Great with coffee in the morning.

As with many French recipes, you'll need time. Your dough goes in and out of the refrigerator 3 times. A full day's work for sure.

Ingredients
1 package dry yeast
¼ cup warm water (110°)
1 cup milk
½ lb butter
1 tablespoon sugar
1 teaspoon salt
3 cups unbleached white flour, sifted
Egg mix (1 yolk and 1 tablespoon milk)

LEAVENING   Soften yeast in warm water and let stand 5 minutes.

BATTER   Scald milk and stir in sugar and salt. Cool to lukewarm. Stir in yeast and add 2 cups of flour, beating vigorously.

KNEADING   Knead in the third cup of flour. It is said that the French give the dough a good solid beating against the bread board about 110 times with the dough held in one hand. Try this way of kneading. The dough should be soft and smooth after it has been kneaded.

RISING   Shape the dough into a smooth ball and place it in a greased bowl. Turn once so greased side is up. Cover with waxed paper and a towel and let rise in a warm place until doubled (1½ hours). Punch down with fist and form into a ball again. Cover and let rise for 30 minutes.

SHAPING   Place butter into a large bowl of ice water. With the hands, break into small portions and squeeze each in water about 20 times or until butter is pliable and waxy. Remove and wipe off excess water. Divide butter into 3 equal portions. Wrap each in waxed paper and chill in refrigerator until firm.

On a lightly floured surface, roll dough into an 18'' square. Dot the middle 6''x 18'' of dough with one portion of butter, cut in small bits. Cover buttered third of dough with right hand third. Fold left hand third of dough under buttered section. With rolling pin, gently press down and seal the upper edges. Wrap dough in waxed paper and chill for 30 minutes.

Remove dough from refrigerator and place on lightly floured surface with buttered section near top, narrow edge of dough toward you. Turn dough ¼ way around, to have open edge away from you, and roll to the original square size. Repeat two more times this procedure of folding, sealing and chilling, using second and third portions of butter.

Finally, place the dough on a floured surface and cut in two. Roll each part into a round ¼'' thick. Cut each round into 12 pie shaped wedges. Roll each wedge up, beginning at the wide end. Fasten the point by brushing with egg mix.

Place rolls on a greased baking sheet with points underneath. Curve the rolls into crescents. Cover lightly with a towel and let rise in a warm place until doubled (45 minutes).

BAKING   Brush with remaining egg mixture and bake at 425° about 20 minutes or until croissants are golden brown. Makes 24 croissants.

Ingredients	1 package dry yeast
	¼ cup warm water
	½ cup milk, scalded
	¼ cup sugar
	¼ cup butter
	½ teaspoon salt
	¼ teaspoon oil of anise
	1 teaspoon ground cinnamon
	3 cups unbleached white flour, sifted
	2 eggs
	2 tablespoons sesame seeds

LEAVENING   Dissolve yeast in warm water and let stand for 5 minutes.

BATTER   Pour hot milk over sugar, butter and salt and stir till butter melts. Cool to lukewarm. Add oil of anise and cinnamon. Mix in thoroughly 1 cup of flour. Add 1 egg and the dissolved yeast, and beat well.

DOUGH   Beat in the remaining flour or enough of it to make a soft dough. Turn out on a lightly floured surface. Cover and let rest 10 minutes.

KNEADING   Knead around 10 minutes or until dough is smooth and elastic, by pushing down and away with heels of hands, folding edges back to center, giving dough a ¼ turn, and so on.

RISING   Form the dough into a ball and place it in a lightly greased bowl, turning once to grease surface. Cover and let rise till doubled (1¼ hours). Punch down and let rise again till almost doubled (1 hour).

SHAPING   Turn dough out on a lightly floured surface and divide in thirds to form balls. Cover and let rest 10 minutes. Roll each part under hands into a strand 16" long, with tapered ends. Line the strands up, 1" apart, on a greased baking sheet. Braid the 3 strands loosely, without stretching dough, beginning at one end. When fully braided, pinch the ends together, cover, and let rise until doubled (40 minutes).

BAKING   Combine 1 slightly beaten egg and 1 tablespoon of water, and brush over the braid. Sprinkle with sesame seeds. Bake at 375° for 25 minutes or until hollow to the tap.

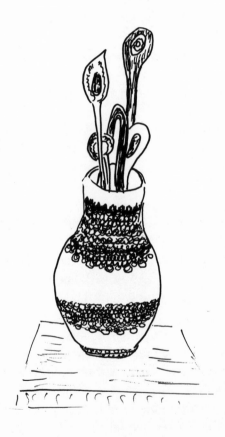

In many countries special breads are baked for holidays like Christmas and New Year. Usually sweet, with plenty of nuts and dried fruits, the breads are sometimes iced and decorated.

Ingredients

2 packages dry yeast
¼ cup warm water
½ cup vegetable oil
¼ cup honey
6¼ cups unbleached white flour
2 eggs
1 cup chopped candied cherries
½ cup chopped walnuts
Icing (½ cup sifted powdered sugar mixed with ¼ teaspoon vanilla and 2 teaspoons milk)
Maraschino cherries, sliced

LEAVENING

Stir yeast into warm water and let stand 5 minutes.

BATTER

Heat milk, oil and honey. Cool to lukewarm, then beat in 2 cups of flour. Beat in eggs one at a time, and add the dissolved yeast. Beat in one more cup of flour until a smooth batter is obtained. Stir in the candied cherries and nuts.

DOUGH

Beat in vigorously 2¼ cups of flour until a soft dough is formed. Reserve the last cup of flour for kneading.

KNEADING

Invert bowl and let dough drop onto lightly floured surface. Knead by pushing dough with heels of the hands, giving dough a ¼ turn, and folding dough back toward center. Repeat until dough is smooth and elastic. If dough sticks to hands add a bit more flour.

RISING   Make dough into a ball and put into a lightly oiled bowl. Turn once to oil top. Cover and let rise in a warm place about 1½ hours or until doubled in bulk.

SHAPING   Punch dough down and divide in 2. Pull each part out to a 24'' log. Join ends together to form circles and place each circle on an oiled cookie sheet. Cover and let rise 40 minutes.

BAKING   Bake at 375° for 20 minutes or until browned. When holiday breads are cool, drizzle icing over them and sprinkle maraschino cherry slices on top.

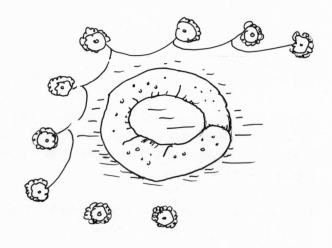

Ingredients	*2 packages dry yeast*
	½ cup warm water
	6 cups unbleached white flour
	½ teaspoon ground anise
	1 cup warm milk
	¼ cup vegetable oil
	¼ cup honey
	¼ cup chopped citron
	¼ cup chopped walnuts
	2 eggs
	Egg mix (1 egg yolk and 1 tablespoon water)

LEAVENING   Stir yeast in warm water and let stand for 5 minutes.

BATTER   Add warm milk to honey and oil. Beat in 2 cups of flour. Add dissolved yeast, 2 beaten eggs, citron and walnuts. Thoroughly beat in 1 more cup of flour until a smooth batter is obtained.

DOUGH   Beat in 2 more cups of flour until a smooth ball of dough is formed.

KNEADING   Knead in the last cup of flour by pressing, turning and folding dough. Knead for about 10 minutes or until the dough is elastic.

RISING   Place dough in oiled bowl, turning to grease top. Cover with waxed paper and towel and let rise in warm place till doubled, 1½ hours.

SHAPING   Punch dough down and divide in 3. Grease two 8" round pans and flatten one piece of dough in each. Make 2 long strands of the remaining piece of dough, and twist one on top of each round piece in any shape you wish. Brush tops with egg mix and let rise 40 minutes.

BAKING   Bake at 375° for 20 minutes, or until a rich brown.

VETEBRÖD (SWEDISH COFFEE BREAD)

The Swedish make lovely shaped coffee breads by braiding, cutting, twisting and otherwise sculpturing the dough.

Ingredients

1 package dry yeast
½ cup warm water
¾ cup warm milk
4 cups unbleached white flour
½ cup honey
½ teaspoon salt
½ cup butter
Cinnamon mix (½ cup sugar and cinnamon)
Egg mix (1 teaspoon water and 1 egg)
¼ cup melted butter

LEAVENING

Dissolve yeast in warm water and let stand for 5 minutes.

BATTER

Melt butter in warm milk and add honey, salt and yeast. Beat in thoroughly 2 cups of flour to form a smooth batter.

DOUGH

Beat in remaining flour to form a soft dough. Allow dough to fall onto lightly floured surface.

KNEADING

Knead by pushing dough with heels of the hands, giving a ¼ turn and folding dough back toward center. Knead for 10 minutes or until the dough is smooth and elastic.

RISING

Form dough into a ball and place in a greased bowl, turning once to grease surface. Cover with waxed paper and a cloth and set aside in a warm place to rise until doubled (1½ hours).

SHAPING   Divide dough in half and roll out each half as thin as possible. Spread with melted butter and cinnamon mix. Roll jelly-roll fashion, beginning at long side and join ends to form a circle. Place each circle on a greased baking sheet. With a scissors cut 1'' in from the edge, at 1½'' intervals, turning the sides of each cut so that spirals of cinnamon show. Let rise about 40 minutes.

BAKING   Brush with egg mix and bake for 15 minutes at 375° or until lightly browned.

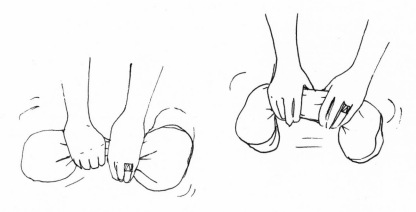

HAMANTASCHEN

In the Book of Esther, Haman was a cruel minister who threatened destruction of the Jews, only to be destroyed himself. Hamantaschen are prepared during Purim, the festival celebrating this deliverance.

Ingredients

1 package dry yeast
1 cup milk
½ cup honey
½ cup oil
5½ cups unbleached white flour
2 eggs
1 egg yolk
Prune filling (1 lb unpitted prunes, ½ cup honey and ½ cup nuts)
Poppy seed filling (12 ounce can of poppy seed)
1 tablespoon lemon juice

LEAVENING

Dissolve yeast in warm water and let stand for 5 minutes.

BATTER

Heat milk, honey, oil and salt and pour into a bowl. Stir in 2 cups of flour and beat well. Add dissolved yeast and 2 eggs, beating vigorously.

DOUGH

Stir in enough flour to make a moderately stiff dough. When dough gets difficult to stir, invert bowl and allow dough to fall on floured board.

KNEADING

Knead in the last of the flour, pushing down and away on the dough with the heels of the hands, folding back the edges, giving a ¼ turn, and repeating. As dough gets moist add a little flour to board. Knead for 10 minutes or until dough is smooth and elastic.

RISING

Shape dough into a ball and place in a greased bowl, turning once to grease top. Cover with waxed paper and towel and let rise in a warm place till doubled (1½ hours).

SHAPING   Punch dough down and divide in half. Roll out each half into a 20''x 12'' rectangle and cut each rectangle into 4'' squares. Place a tablespoon of prune or poppy seed filling in center of each square. Bring 2 opposing corners together to form a triangle, moisten edges and pinch them together to seal.

FILLING   For prune filling, rinse 2 cups unpitted prunes (1 lb) and cover with water to a depth of 1 inch above fruit in saucepan. Cover and simmer gently for 15 minutes. Drain, remove pits and chop prunes. Add ½ cup honey, ½ cup nuts and 1 tablespoon lemon juice. Mix well.
For poppy seed filling, combine 12 ounce can of poppy seed with 1 tablespoon of lemon juice.

BAKING   Place filled Hamantaschen on a greased baking sheet. Cover loosely and let rise till doubled (30 minutes). Brush tops with egg yolk combined with a tablespoon of water. Bake at 350° for 15 minutes or until nicely browned.

SERVING   Remove from sheet and cool. Excellent with tea. Makes 30 servings.

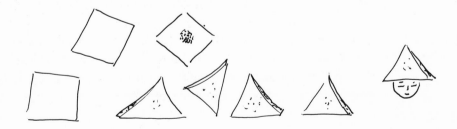

DANISH PASTRY

Start your Danish pastry the night before by creaming a cup of butter with a ½ cup of sifted flour, rolling between waxed paper to a 13''x 6'' rectangle, and chilling overnight in refrigerator.

Ingredients

2 packages dry yeast
½ cup warm water
¾ cup milk
¼ cup honey
1 cup butter (see above)
4¼ cups unbleached white flour, sifted
1 teaspoon salt
1 egg
Prune filling (¾ cup cooked prunes, ¼ cup honey, 1 tablespoon corn-
    starch)
Nut filling (¾ cup chopped nuts, ½ cup butter, ¼ cup brown sugar)

LEAVENING

Dissolve yeast in ½ cup warm water and let stand 5 minutes.

BATTER

Heat milk, honey and salt till just warm. In a large bowl, beat together the milk mixture, dissolved yeast and 3½ cups of flour.

DOUGH

Stir in thoroughly the last ¾ cup of flour to make a soft dough.

KNEADING

Invert bowl and allow dough to fall on lightly floured surface. Knead for about 10 minutes by pushing down and away with heels of the hands, folding edges of dough in toward center, giving dough ¼ turn, and so on until the dough is smooth and elastic.

RISING

Form dough into ball and place in a lightly greased bowl, turning once to grease top. Cover with waxed paper and a towel and set aside in a warm place to rise until doubled (1½ hours).

SHAPING   On a lightly floured board, roll dough out to a 14" square. Place the refrigerated flour-butter sheet on half the dough and fold over the other half, sealing the edges. Roll the folded dough out and fold it again in thirds. Repeat the rolling out and folding three times. If the butter softens place dough in refrigerator to chill. After final rolling, chill for 30 minutes.

Divide dough into 3 parts. Roll each part into a 12"x 9" rectangle, then cut it into 3" squares (36 in all). Place 1 teaspoon of filling in the center of each square and fold four corners to meet and overlap slightly in the center, enclosing the filling.

FILLING   For prune filling, thoroughly mix prunes, honey and cornstarch.
For nut filling, cream the butter and brown sugar, then add nuts.

BAKING   Place pastries on ungreased baking sheet, cover and let rise in a warm place till doubled (45 minutes). Bake for 10 minutes at 425°.

Ingredients

½ *cup scalded milk*
2 *tablespoons sugar*
1 *teaspoon salt*
2 *tablespoons butter*
¼ *cup warm water*
1 *package dry yeast*
1 *egg well beaten*
3 *cups unbleached white flour, sifted*
Filling:
½ *teaspoon cinnamon*
½ *cup finely chopped black walnuts*
¼ *cup melted butter*
2 *tablespoons brown sugar*

LEAVENING

Stir yeast into warm water and let stand for 5 minutes.

BATTER

Scald milk, remove from heat and add sugar, salt and butter. Stir until butter is melted. Add water, egg and dissolved yeast. Blend thoroughly, adding flour a cup at a time.

DOUGH

The last cup of flour should produce a smooth, soft dough. If it is sticky, add a bit more flour. Invert bowl and allow dough to fall on a lightly floured board.

KNEADING

With floured hands, knead dough about 8 minutes. Push dough with heels of hands, give dough a ¼ turn clockwise, fold dough and repeat until dough is satiny.

RISING

Form dough into a ball and put into an oiled bowl. Turn once to oil top. Cover with waxed paper and a towel and put into a warm place to rise for about 1½ hours or until doubled in bulk.

SHAPING   Punch the dough down and roll out into an oblong ¼'' thick. Spread
               with the mixture of melted butter, cinnamon, brown sugar and nuts.
               Fold dough over like a jelly roll and cut into 1½'' slices.

BAKING   Place the rolls on a large, greased cookie sheet. Brush tops with soft-
               ened butter. Cover and let rise to double (about 45 minutes). Bake in
               preheated 425° oven about 20 minutes or until rolls are golden brown.

SERVING   Rolls should be served warm. They may be reheated later by brushing
               tops with melted butter and baking for 5 minutes at 400°.

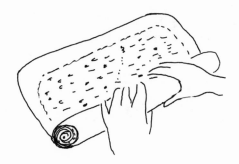

Quick

Breads

The word *muffin* is derived from the old French *moufflet* meaning soft bread. Muffins are simple to make and provide a tasty hot bread for breakfast. The basic recipe lends itself to many variations.

Ingredients

2 cups unbleached white flour
2 teaspoons baking powder
½ teaspoon salt
¼ cup maple syrup
1 egg
¼ cup vegetable oil
¾ cup milk

BATTER

Have two bowls ready. Mix flour, baking powder and salt in one. In the other beat the egg, then add oil and milk. Make a well in the flour and all at once pour in the wet ingredients. Mix until dry ingredients are completely wet. Do not overmix.

SHAPING

Spoon the batter into greased muffin tins until two thirds full.

BAKING

Bake at 350° for about 20 minutes or until well risen and golden brown.

SERVING

Remove from tins gently. Serve hot, with butter.

Variations on New England muffins involve some simple changes in the basic recipe.

BLUEBERRY MUFFINS Follow the recipe until all ingredients are mixed. Then fold in 1 cup of fresh blueberries and continue the recipe.

APPLE MUFFINS When all the ingredients have been mixed for New England muffins, fold in the following: 1 cup diced apples mixed with 1 tablespoon sugar and 1 teaspoon cinnamon. Then continue with the recipe.

WHEAT GERM MUFFINS Substitute ½ cup wheat germ for ½ cup unbleached white flour, and substitute ¼ cup honey for ¼ cup maple syrup, then proceed with the recipe.

CORN MEAL MUFFINS Substitute 1 cup corn meal for 1 cup unbleached white flour and proceed with the recipe.

CORN BREAD   Here's a native American recipe that is simple enough for a child to have fun with.

Ingredients
1 lb corn meal
Boiling water
½ cup molasses

BATTER   Add enough boiling water to the corn meal and molasses so that it will hold together as you stir.

SHAPING   When cool enough to handle, shape into a greased loaf pan.

BAKING   Bake slowly (325°) for 1 hour.

BEAN BREAD   Addition of soybeans makes for a nutritious bread.

Ingredients
1 lb soybeans
2 cups corn meal
½ teaspoon salt
½ teaspoon baking powder
½ teaspoon baking soda
½ cup molasses

BATTER   Put beans in pot with enough water to cover. Bring to a boil and simmer for 4 hours. Mix corn meal, salt, baking powder and soda in a bowl, then pour simmering beans and the molasses over the meal mix.

SHAPING   When cool enough to touch, mold into a greased bread pan.

BAKING   Bake for 1 hour at 350°.

CORN PONES

A popular southern small bread. The word *pone* is derived from the Algonquian *ăpân* which means "bread".

Ingredients

1½ cups water
2¼ cups corn meal
½ teaspoon baking soda
½ cup buttermilk
1 teaspoon salt

BATTER

Add corn meal to boiling water. Add the remaining ingredients, mixing thoroughly, until batter coheres.

SHAPING

Shape between palms into 10 oval pones, 1'' thick.

BAKING

Place pones on a greased cookie sheet and bake until brown in a 400° oven.

Originally "journey cake" for the long wagon haul.

Ingredients

½ cup unbleached white flour
1½ cups corn meal
2 tablespoons maple syrup
2 tablespoons oil
2 teaspoons baking soda
½ cup milk
½ cup sour cream
1 egg

BATTER

Beat egg, then add oil, milk, sour cream and maple syrup. In another bowl combine all dry ingredients: flour, corn meal, baking soda. Make a well in the center of the dry ingredients and pour in the wet ingredients. Mix thoroughly until batter is smooth.

SHAPING

Pour into greased 8" square pan.

BAKING

Bake at 400° for 30 minutes.

SERVING

Slice into squares and serve warm with butter and maple syrup or honey.

BOSTON BROWN BREAD

This dark bread originated in England where it was known as brown bread. It was made of coarse, unsifted wheat flour, or of maslin, a mixture of grains.

Ingredients

1 cup unbleached white flour
1 teaspoon baking powder
1 teaspoon soda
1 teaspoon salt
½ cup cornmeal
1½ cups whole wheat flour
¾ cup molasses
2 cups buttermilk

BATTER

Mix white flour with baking powder, soda and salt. Stir in the cornmeal and whole wheat flour. Add remaining ingredients and beat well until a smooth batter is formed.

SHAPING

Divide batter among 4 greased and floured 1 lb food cans. Cover tightly with foil.

STEAMING AND BAKING

Place the cans on a rack in a deep kettle. Pour in boiling water to a 1'' depth and cover the kettle. Steam for 3 hours, adding more water if needed. Uncover cans and place them in a very hot oven (450°) for 5 minutes. Remove breads from cans and cool on a rack.

SERVING

Wrap and store the breads overnight before serving. Traditionally served with baked beans.

Ingredients	*1¾ cups unbleached white flour*
	½ cup rolled oats
	1 teaspoon baking soda
	1 egg
	¼ teaspoon salt
	2 tablespoons melted butter
	½ cup milk
	Egg mix (1 egg yolk and 1 teaspoon milk)
DOUGH	Sift flour, baking soda and salt into a bowl. In another bowl, beat the egg, add oats, milk and butter. Make a well in the flour mixture and pour the wet ingredients in, mixing vigorously until a dough forms.
KNEADING	Turn dough onto lightly floured surface and knead quickly (2 minutes) until it holds together in a smooth ball.
SHAPING	Roll to ½" thickness. With a cookie cutter or top of a floured drinking glass, cut into 2" circles (about 16). Place circles on a greased cookie sheet and brush egg mix on top of each.
BAKING	Bake for 15 minutes in a 400° oven or until brown on top.
SERVING	May be served immediately with butter or allowed to cool before serving.

Popovers should arrive at the table piping hot, puffed up and ready for buttering. Start them ½ hour before dinner time.

Ingredients

1 cup unbleached white flour
1 cup milk
2 eggs
¼ teaspoon salt
2 tablespoons vegetable oil

BATTER

Have 2 bowls ready. In one place the flour and salt. In the other beat the eggs until light and foamy. Stir in milk and oil, then add the wet ingredients all at once to the flour and beat together for about a minute.

SHAPING

Pour the batter into greased custard cups until half full, or for smaller popovers, half fill muffin tins.

BAKING

Place in a preheated oven set at 450°. Bake for 15 minutes or until popovers are puffed. Then reduce heat to 350° and bake about 25 minutes or until well browned. Prick tops with a toothpick to allow steam to escape.

SERVING

Serve hot. Makes 7 large or 12 small popovers.

A meal in itself, quickly made, in the dumpling family.

Ingredients
2 cups yellow corn meal
1½ teaspoons salt
2½ cups water
2 cups milk, scalded
1 onion, finely chopped
1 clove garlic, finely chopped
½ cup melted butter
2 eggs lightly beaten
½ cup grated Cheddar cheese
¼ cup grated Parmesan cheese
1 tablespoon chopped chives
1 teaspoon sweet basil

BATTER
Mix the corn meal, salt and water together in the top of a double boiler. Stir in the scalded milk and cook for about 15 minutes over boiling water until it comes to a boil. Stir frequently.

Meanwhile cook the onion and garlic in 2 tablespoons of butter until tender but not browned. Add to the cooked corn meal mixture.

Beat in the eggs and Cheddar cheese and spread the mixture into a greased pan or dish, so that is about ½ inch thick.

SHAPING
Cool mixture to room temperature. Cut it into squares, diamonds or round shapes, and arrange, slightly overlapping, in a greased heatproof dish.

BROILING
Pour over the remaining butter, sprinkle with chives and sweet basil and Parmesan, and heat under a preheated broiler until hot throughout and lightly browned on top.

Quick
Sweet
Breads

A traditional recipe with plenty of healthful ingredients.

Ingredients

2½ cups unbleached white flour
½ teaspoon soda
2 teaspoons baking powder
½ teaspoon salt
1½ teaspoons ginger
2 teaspoons cinnamon
½ teaspoon ground cloves
1 cup warm water
2 beaten eggs
1 cup molasses
½ cup oil

BATTER

Have two bowls ready. In one combine all dry ingredients, and in the other all the wet. Gradually merge the two, beating until the batter is smooth.

BAKING

Pour the batter into a greased, square baking pan and bake at 325° for 45 minutes or until an inserted toothpick comes out clean. Remove from oven and let stand 5 minutes.

SERVING

Cut into squares and serve warm. May be topped with whipped cream.

GERMAN KUCHEN

Ingredients	*½ cup oil*
	½ cup maple syrup
	2 egg yolks
	1½ cups unbleached white flour
	2 teaspoons baking powder
	½ teaspoon salt
	½ cup milk
	2 stiffly beaten egg whites
	Topping (½ cup white flour, ¼ cup brown sugar, 2 tablespoons butter)

BATTER Have two bowls ready. In one first mix oil and maple syrup, then beat in egg yolks and stir in milk. In the other bowl sift together flour, baking powder and salt. Beat the wet ingredients thoroughly into the dry ingredients. Fold in the egg whites.

TOPPING Mix together ½ cup flour and ¼ cup brown sugar, and cut in 2 tablespoons of softened butter.

SHAPING Pour the batter into a greased 9'' square pan. Sprinkle topping over batter.

BAKING Bake at 350° for 30 minutes.

SERVING Cut into squares and serve warm. Usually served with coffee.

Ingredients

2 teaspoons baking powder
½ teaspoon salt
¼ cup softened butter
½ cup honey
1 beaten egg
½ cup milk
1½ cups unbleached white flour, sifted
½ cup chopped peanuts
2 tablespoons melted butter
2 teaspoons cinnamon
½ cup brown sugar
2 tablespoons flour

BATTER

In a bowl blend butter, egg and honey. Mix in milk. Blend baking powder, flour and salt, and beat into the wet mixture until smooth.

SHAPING

Pour half the batter into a greased baking pan. In a cup combine brown sugar, cinnamon and 2 tablespoons of flour. Sprinkle half of this mixture evenly over the batter in the pan. Pour the second half of the batter into the same pan over the first half. Combine peanuts and melted butter with the remaining brown sugar-cinnamon, and sprinkle over the batter.

BAKING

Bake at 350° for around 35 minutes. Remove pan and let stand for 5 minutes. Cut into 6 portions.

Ingredients

½ cup oil
3 eggs
1 cup nuts (walnuts and almonds)
¾ cup sugar
1 teaspoon almond extract
2½ cups unbleached white flour
1 teaspoon baking powder
1 teaspoon cinnamon
¼ cup candied fruit (optional)

BATTER

Have 2 bowls ready. In one, beat together oil, ½ cup sugar and eggs, either manually or by electric mixer. Add almond extract and chopped nuts. In another bowl, join flour and baking powder, then mix slowly into wet ingredients and beat until smooth. If desired, candied fruit may be added into the batter.

SHAPING

Divide batter into 3 parts on a board. Sprinkle flour on a greased cookie sheet, and shape each section with floured hands into a 1½'' thick tapered loaf. Sprinkle with a mix of ¼ cup sugar and cinnamon.

BAKING

Bake at 350° for 30 minutes. Remove and cut each bread diagonally into thin slices. Return to oven set at 400° for 5 minutes.

Ingredients

2½ cups unbleached white flour
½ cup sugar
3 teaspoons baking powder
½ teaspoon salt
2 beaten eggs
1 cup milk
2 tablespoons vegetable oil
¼ cup finely diced maraschino cherries
¼ cup diced dates
½ cup chopped walnuts
Optional icing (½ cup sifted powdered sugar mixed with
    ¼ teaspoon vanilla and 2 teaspoons milk)

BATTER

Have two bowls ready. In one sift together flour, sugar, baking powder and salt. In another combine eggs, milk and oil. Add the wet ingredients to the flour mixture, beating well to form a smooth batter. Stir in fruits and nuts.

SHAPING

Pour the batter into a greased 9" loaf pan.

BAKING

Bake at 350° for 45 minutes or until an inserted toothpick comes out clean. Remove from pan and cool on a rack.

SERVING

If desired, drizzle icing over the bread. Slice thin and serve plain or with butter.

BLACK FOREST APPLE STRUDEL

Ingredients

3 cups unbleached white flour
¼ lb butter
5 tablespoons vegetable oil (2 for brushing)
1 egg
2 tablespoons cold water
Dash of salt
½ cup brown sugar
1½ cups diced fresh apples
1 teaspoon cinnamon
1 cup chopped walnuts

DOUGH

Cut butter and 3 tablespoons of oil into flour with fork until blended. Add egg and water. Gather dough together into a ball and work it with the hands until smooth.

SHAPING

Divide dough into 4 balls, cover with waxed paper and refrigerate for 2 hours. Then flatten and roll each ball between two sheets of waxed paper to the thinnest square possible. It may be necessary to cut and patch to make a square. Brush tops with oil. Mix sugar, apples, cinnamon and chopped walnuts, and spread over the surface of the squares, keeping away from the edges. Roll up jelly roll fashion.

BAKING

Place on greased cookie sheet and bake for 40 minutes at 350° or until golden brown.

SERVING

Slice while still warm. Serve cool with coffee or tea.

Ingredients	3 cups unbleached white flour, sifted
	7 tablespoons cold water
	½ cup brown sugar
	¾ cup vegetable oil
	¼ cup melted butter
	½ cup maple syrup

DOUGH

Mix water and vegetable oil and add all at once to flour. Stir lightly with a fork, then work into a smooth ball by hand. If more water is needed, add by the teaspoon, only as much as is necessary.

SHAPING

Divide dough into 6 balls. Flatten each ball and roll out, between 2 sheets of waxed paper, to a paper thin 8'' square. It may be necessary to cut and patch to make the square. Set each square aside on waxed paper as it is made.

Brush melted butter on bottom of 8''x 8'' pan and invert one wax-papered square of dough into the pan, peeling away the paper. Mix brown sugar, melted butter and walnuts together and spread on this first layer of dough. Place second square of dough over the first, and spread again with nut mix. Repeat until all 6 squares are used. Pour enough maple syrup to cover the top. Cut baklawah diagonally to make an X, then cut a + from left to right and top to bottom, so dividing it into 8 triangles.

BAKING

Bake for 45 minutes in oven set at 325°. If baklawah becomes dry, pour more syrup to cover top. Baklawah should be rich golden brown.

SERVING

Serve cool. Covered with saran wrap or foil, the baklawah should remain fresh for many days.

Flat

Breads

CHAPATTY

A simple bread served widely in India and Nepal that goes well with rice and vegetable meals, or with yoghurt dishes.

Ingredients
½ cup unbleached white flour
1 cup whole wheat flour
¼ cup water

DOUGH
Make a well in the flour and pour water into it. Mix thoroughly until dough holds together. More water may be needed, but add sparingly until dough can be formed into a ball.

KNEADING
Press down with the hands, fold dough and knead for a few minutes until it has a smooth feeling.

RISING
Cover with a damp towel and let rest for 20 minutes.

SHAPING
Form into 8 balls. With floured hands, clap each ball until it is somewhat flattened. Turn onto floured surface. Continue flattening with the hands until a 6'' circle is formed.

BAKING
Bake on a heated, ungreased iron skillet for a few minutes. Turn to brown other side. Chapatties will puff out.

SERVING
Serve hot.

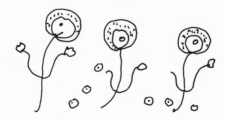

INDIAN PURIS (FRIED BREAD)

Ingredients	*2½ cups whole wheat flour*
	2 tablespoons melted butter (ghee)
	¾ cup warm water
	Oil for frying

DOUGH

In one bowl mix butter with warm water. In another put the whole wheat flour. Make a well in the center of the flour and pour in water. Mix vigorously with a wooden spoon until a smooth ball is formed.

KNEADING

Invert bowl and allow dough to fall onto lightly floured surface. Knead by pushing down with the heels of the hands, folding dough, and giving a ¼ turn. Knead about 5 minutes or until dough is smooth and elastic. Cover dough with a damp cloth and set aside for 30 minutes.

SHAPING

Form dough into 8 balls 2" in diameter and flatten them out with floured hands. Roll out to 7" circles, adding flour if dough gets sticky. Cover circles with damp towel and set aside for 10 minutes.

FRYING

Fry in deep hot oil in a small wock or a heavy skillet. Put puris in the pan one at a time. They will immediately bubble out and rise to the top. Press down with slotted spatula and fry for 2 minutes, then turn over and fry on other side for 2 more minutes or until lightly browned, pressing down with spatula.

SERVING

Remove puris gently from hot oil with tongs, allowing oil to drip back into pan, and place on absorbent towel. Just before serving, brush puris with melted butter, stack 3 to a pile on a cookie sheet, and heat for 5 minutes at 350°. Serve hot, with a spiced Indian vegetable dish.

Like most breads of India the paratha is unleavened and of wheat flour. The paratha is sometimes filled with spiced mashed potatoes before baking.

Ingredients

1½ cups whole wheat flour
¾ cup cold water
10 tablespoons melted butter (ghee)
Optional potato filling:
1 cup mashed potatoes
1 hot pepper
1 tablespoon coriander
1 minced onion

DOUGH

Combine flour and 1 tablespoon of butter in a bowl. Work flour and butter together until they are mealy to the touch. Pour ½ cup of water over the flour mixture, kneading vigorously until a dough is formed. Gather dough into a ball. If particles of dough crumble, add up to ¼ cup more water, a few drops at a time.

KNEADING

Knead by pressing down the dough with the heels of the hands, folding back the edges, giving a ¼ turn, and repeating. Knead for 8 minutes or until the dough is smooth and elastic. Gather the dough into a ball, place it in a bowl, and drape a kitchen towel over the top. Let the dough rest at least 30 minutes before rolling it.

SHAPING

Break off a sixth of the dough, and on a lightly floured surface roll it into a 7'' round. With the fingers brush the top with ½ teaspoon butter. If desired, a tablespoon of filling may be spread on the top at this point. Fold the round in half and again brush the top with ½ teaspoon of butter. Fold the half-round once more to make a four-layered quarter circle. With the rolling pin press the layers together lightly, flattening the paratha somewhat. Repeating the process, roll and shape the other

5 parathas in a similar fashion. Parathas may be covered with a damp cloth and kept at room temperature for 3 or 4 hours before they are fried.

FILLING

Optional filling: Mince pepper and combine with potatoes, coriander, onion. Place 1 tablespoon filling on each paratha before folding.

BAKING

Heat a well seasoned cast iron skillet so that a drop of water put on its surface dances immediately. Place one of the parathas in the pan, moving it constantly with a wooden paddle or the fingers until specks of brown begin to appear on the surface. Turn paratha and spread melted butter on top. Cook for 2 minutes, turn again, spread with another teaspoon of butter, and cook for one more minute. Cover parathas with foil and keep in a warm oven while the remaining parathas are being baked. Depending on the size of the skillet, 2 or 3 parathas may be fried at a time.

SERVING

Serve the parathas warm with a meal. They are traditionally accompanied by unflavored yoghurt. Parathas may be cooked ahead of time and reheated in an ungreased skillet for a minute on each side. Makes 6 servings.

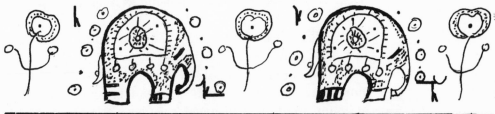

Tortillas are the traditional breads of Mexican Indians. Pounded and rolled into flat round shapes and filled with meat, vegetables and spices, tortillas are a piquant meal-in-one.

Ingredients	*1½ cups unbleached white flour* *1 cup yellow corn meal* *½ teaspoon salt* *1¼ cups water*
DOUGH	Blend flour, corn meal and salt. Stir in just enough water so that the particles adhere into a ball of dough.
KNEADING	Knead and pound the dough on a floured surface until it is smooth and elastic. Form into a ball. Cover with a damp towel and let rest for 10 minutes.
SHAPING	Break into 1'' balls and roll into thin circles.
BAKING	Bake on a heated skillet, turning tortillas so that both sides are lightly flecked with brown. Flip tortillas out onto a warm dish or stack on a cookie sheet in a warm oven until all tortillas have been made.
SALAD FILLING	Left-over salad diced fine and spiced with chili powder, garlic and onions is a good choice for a filling.
STEAK FILLING	Quickly stir-fry ½ lb. round steak diced thin, 1 diced onion, 1 diced green pepper, salt, pepper, chili powder to taste.
MEATBALL FILLING	Crush 6 small cooked meatballs with diced green peppers and onions. Heat for 10 minutes in tomato sauce.

TOSTADAS   To make tostadas simply follow the recipe for Mexican rolled tortillas, placing each cooked tortilla as it comes from the skillet, onto an oiled cookie sheet. Bake for 15 minutes at 350°. Remove and stack on a cloth napkin, 5 or 6 to a stack. The filling is put on top of the tostada which is eaten flat, without folding.

ENCHILADAS   To make enchiladas, follow the recipe for Mexican rolled tortillas, but cook the tortillas on one side only. Remove the half-cooked tortilla to an absorbent towel. Place 1 tablespoon of filling on the cooked side of the tortilla and fold like an envelope. Place the enchiladas on an oblong baking pan. Cover with tomato sauce sprinkled with grated cheese and dried chives. Cover with foil and bake for 20 minutes at 325°.

Ingredients

1¾ cups unbleached white flour
¾ cup boiling water
1 tablespoon vegetable oil

DOUGH

Mix flour and boiling water in a bowl, using a wooden spoon, until a dough is formed.

KNEADING

When the dough cools enough to handle, knead it for about 3 minutes or until it forms a smooth ball. Cover with a wet towel and set aside for 30 minutes.

SHAPING

With your hands pull and shape the dough into a 12'' log. On a lightly floured surface roll the log until it is smooth and even. Cut into 1'' slices. With the palm of the hand flatten each slice into a circle and roll out into a thin 7'' circle with a rolling pin.

FRYING

Fry the pancakes on a medium hot griddle, one side only, until light brown (1 minute). Remove and brush oil on unfried side. Stack and cover with a towel.

STEAMING

Just before serving, steam in layers of 3 on a steaming tier or on top of boiling rice, with foil to separate, for 10 minutes.

SERVING

Traditionally served with Peking duck. Mandarin pancakes are stacked on the table, covered with a towel. Vegetable filling or pieces of duck are placed on the pancake which is eaten rolled up like a scroll.

PERSIAN NANE SAJ (NOMAD BREAD)

Nomadic tribes of Persia (Iran) bake an unleavened wheat bread (nan) on a curved metal plate (saj) over hot stones.

Ingredients
4 cups whole wheat flour
¾ cup warm water

DOUGH
Stir water into flour and mix thoroughly.

KNEADING
Turn dough onto lightly floured surface. To knead, press down on the dough with the heels of the hands, giving dough a ¼ turn, and fold dough toward center. Knead for 5 minutes, adding a little flour if dough sticks, until a smooth ball of dough is formed. Let rest 10 minutes.

SHAPING
Shape into 2'' balls (about 10) and press with hands into thin circles. Press and turn with the hands until each circle is about 10'' across.

BAKING
Place 2 circles at a time on a cookie sheet and bake for 5 minutes in a 475° oven. For a more authentic look bake each circle over a curved metal surface such as an inverted small wock.

The Hebrew word *matsah* means "pressed". Matzohs are unleavened breads that the Israelis baked on their exodus across the desert from Egypt. They are traditionally eaten by Jews at the Passover holiday. Commercially prepared matzohs are precise, perforated machine made sheets. To bring back the flavor of ancient times and to taste matzohs as they might have been at the time of Moses, try the following.

Ingredients

2 cups whole wheat flour
¾ cup warm water

DOUGH

Mix flour with only as much water as necessary to form a cohesive ball.

KNEADING

With floured hands knead by pressing down on the dough, giving a ¼ turn, folding dough over, and repeating until the dough is smooth, about 10 minutes. Cover with a damp cloth and set aside in a warm place for 35 minutes.

SHAPING

With the hands, roll dough into a long snake about 1½" in diameter. Cut into 10 pieces. Place each piece on a floured surface, pressing and patting until it becomes a flat circle. Cover with a damp cloth and set aside for 10 minutes. Before baking, score matzohs with the tines of a fork.

BAKING

Have a hot, dry griddle ready. Bake each matzoh for about 2 minutes on both sides, or until lightly browned. For crispier matzohs, bake 4 at a time on an ungreased cookie sheet, for 4 minutes in an oven set at 475°.

SERVING

Matzohs may be served with any meal. For storing, place in plastic bags.

EGG
MATZOHS

2 cups whole wheat flour
1 cup unbleached white flour
1 cup warm water
1 tablespoon honey
1 egg
Pinch salt

DOUGH

Mix wheat and white flour in a bowl. In another bowl beat the egg, then add water, honey and salt. Make a well in the flour and add the egg mix all at once. Stir vigorously until the dough coheres into a ball.

KNEADING

Let the dough fall onto a lightly floured surface and knead for 10 minutes by pushing down on dough with heels of the hands, folding dough back and giving it a ¼ turn. When dough is smooth, cover with a damp cloth and set aside for 30 minutes.

SHAPING

Pull dough to a 1½'' diameter log. Cut into 12 pieces. By hand pat each piece out into a flat circle. Score with tines of a fork for easy breaking.

BAKING

Bake 4 at a time on an ungreased cookie sheet, for 5 minutes in a 475° oven.

SERVING

Cool and serve with butter or jam. May be stored in plastic bags.

TIBETAN BREAD

A primitive bread with chewy crust. Good jaw exercise, excellent taste.

Ingredients

2 cups barley flour
2 cups unbleached white flour
2 cups whole wheat flour
1 cup sesame seeds
1 teaspoon salt
4 tablespoons vegetable oil
3½ cups boiling water

*BATTER
AND
DOUGH*

Mix sesame seeds with the barley flour and pan roast in 1 tablespoon of oil until darkened. Mix all of the flours together, adding salt. Add the remaining 3 tablespoons of oil to the boiling water and pour into the flour, beating vigorously with a wooden spoon until the dough begins to form.

KNEADING

When cool to the touch, turn out on a lightly floured board and knead for 10 minutes or until smooth and elastic. Knead by pushing down and away with heels of the hands, folding edges back to center, giving a ¼ turn, and so on.

SHAPING

Place dough in an oiled bread pan and score the top lengthwise with a knife. Refrigerate overnight.

BAKING

Bake at 400° for 1 hour, then reduce heat to 350° and bake for 20 minutes longer.

TIBETAN BARLEY BALLS

Barley is the staple grain of Tibet. Tibetans will knead barley flour into a dough and eat it with a strong buttered tea brewed from bricks of tea leaves and roots. In the recipe, white flour has been added to make the barley balls more congenial to western taste. For the true Tibetan taste use barley flour alone.

Ingredients
1 cup roasted barley flour
1 cup unbleached white flour
1 cup hot water
¼ lb butter

DOUGH   Mix barley and white flour together thoroughly. Melt butter in hot water and add to the flour all at once, mixing vigorously. Particles of dough will flake off. Gather them back and press them into the ball of dough. Cover with a damp towel and set aside for 30 minutes.

KNEADING   With flour on the hands, knead dough by pressing and turning, gathering particles of dough at the same time. Knead until the dough is fairly smooth, about 4 minutes.

SHAPING   Break the dough into 1'' balls, about 20 in all. Cover with a damp towel and let rest for 10 minutes.

COOKING   Drop balls one at a time into a large pot of boiling clear soup. Reduce to medium heat when all balls are in the pot, cover and cook for 20 minutes.

SERVING   Serve the barley balls in the hot soup or as a side dish with vegetables and meat.

Maize is a staple food of much of Africa. Agidi is a corn meal dumpling wrapped and boiled in banana leaves.

Ingredients

2 cups corn meal
2½ cups boiling water
12 large cabbage leaves
Optional sweet and sour sauce:
¼ cup catsup
2 tablespoons honey
Juice of ½ lemon
2 tablespoons soy sauce
1 chopped onion
½ cup yellow raisins
2 cups boiling water

DOUGH

Pour just enough boiling water over the corn meal so that it holds together in one piece as you mix. When mixture cools enough to handle, turn out onto corn mealed surface.

SHAPING

Boil cabbage leaves for 20 minutes. Meanwhile, divide dough into 12 parts and with corn mealed hands shape each part into a finger 4'' long and 1'' in diameter. Put each finger into a boiled cabbage leaf and roll up like a scroll.

COOKING

Place agidi in a large shallow pan, with ends of leaves on bottom, adding just enough water to cover. Cook for 20 minutes. Add more water if necessary. For more pungency (although this is *not* Nigerian), make a sweet and sour sauce of catsup, honey, lemon juice, soy sauce, chopped onion, and raisins all boiled in 2 cups of water. Pour the sauce over the agidi, adding water if needed, and cook 20 minutes.

SERVING

Serve hot as a bread or as a side dish with meats or vegetables.

Pancakes

Ingredients

1 cup unbleached white flour
2½ teaspoons baking powder
½ teaspoon salt
1 beaten egg
¾ cup milk
2 tablespoons vegetable oil

BATTER

Combine flour with baking powder and salt. Stir milk into beaten egg and combine all at once with the dry ingredients.

BAKING

Spoon 3 or 4 mounds of batter onto large hot griddle and bake until bubbles appear on the surface. Turn to brown other side.

SERVING

Serve hot with syrup and butter.

FRENCH PANCAKES (CREPES)

Ingredients	*3 eggs*
	1 teaspoon salt
	1 cup unbleached white flour
	1¼ cups milk
	1 tablespoon melted butter

BATTER   Beat eggs until foamy. Add milk, then slowly add to flour and salt, mixing thoroughly.

BAKING   Have a small buttered, heated pan ready. Pour in enough batter to cover the bottom, tipping if necessary to spread batter thinly and evenly. Brown on one side. When top is set, turn pancake and bake for 2 minutes or until brown.

SERVING   Sprinkle with powdered sugar, roll into jelly-roll, serve warm.

GERMAN PANCAKES

Ingredients	*3 eggs*
	1 teaspoon salt
	¾ cup unbleached white flour
	¾ cup milk
	2 tablespoons softened butter

BATTER   Mix eggs by hand or mixer until light yellow in color. Add remaining ingredients and mix until smooth.

BAKING   Have 2 greased 8" baking dishes ready. Pour batter into each dish and bake for about 10 minutes at 400°, then reduce heat to 350° and bake for 10 more minutes.

SERVING   Serve on hot plate with lemon slices, powdered sugar and butter.

Ingredients

2 eggs, well beaten
1¼ cups unbleached white flour
1 cup milk
3 tablespoons maple syrup
A few pinches of salt
1 cup beer
3 teaspoons unsalted butter
1 cup applesauce
¼ cup sour cream or yoghurt

BATTER

Mix eggs, flour, milk, 1 tablespoon maple syrup and salt to make a smooth pancake batter. Let the batter rest for 1½ hours. Stir in the beer at the last moment, just before cooking the pancakes.

BAKING

Heat an 8'' frying pan. When the pan is hot add ¼ teaspoon of butter. Let the butter melt and cover the bottom of the pan. Pour a ladle of batter into the pan and gently tip the pan so that batter covers the bottom. When the batter bubbles, turn the pancake over and cook for 4 or 5 seconds longer. Flip the pancake into a buttered deep 8'' baking dish (round, heatproof glass is good). Repeat until the batter is all used, adding butter to pan before baking each pancake.

Drip melted butter and applesauce over each layer to a depth of 12 pancakes. On the very top spread the remaining applesauce and a mixture of 2 tablespoons of maple syrup and ¼ cup sour cream or yoghurt. Dot with butter. Bake in oven at 350° for 20 minutes.

BLINTZES

Ingredients

2 well beaten eggs
½ cup unbleached white flour
1 teaspoon salt
½ cup milk
¼ cup water
Filling:
1 lb creamed cottage cheese
½ teaspoon salt
1 tablespoon sugar
1 egg
½ teaspoon cinnamon
1 teaspoon cornstarch

BATTER

In one bowl combine flour with salt. In another, mix milk, water and beaten eggs. Make a well in the flour and pour the wet ingredients into it, mixing until smooth. Batter will be thin.

FIRST FRYING

Oil bottom of a small skillet and heat over medium heat. Pour enough batter to cover bottom of the pan and tilt pan so that batter spreads evenly. When edges begin to curl and turn brown, invert pan and let shell fall onto clean towel. Repeat until all shells are made.

FILLING AND SHAPING

Combine all ingredients for the filling, and place 1 tablespoon in the center of the browned side of each shell. Fold the shell around the filling, envelope fashion, and set aside until ready to fry. Blintzes may be frozen at this point, if desired.

SECOND FRYING

Fry 4 or 5 blintzes at once on a well oiled large skillet, with folded side down. Turn once to brown both sides.

SERVING

Serve hot, plain or with berries and sour cream.

Ingredients	*1 cup unbleached white flour*
	¾ cup yellow corn meal
	¼ teaspoon salt
	1 egg
	1¾ cups water

BATTER

Mix unbleached flour, corn meal and salt. Add egg and water and beat thoroughly with rotary beater until batter is smooth and quite liquid.

BAKING

Pour 2 tablespoons of batter into a hot, greased 6'' skillet, tilting to cover bottom evenly. Cook until sides curl and top is just set (about 2 minutes). Turn once and cook for 1 minute on other side. Flip onto paper towel.

CHICKEN OR MEAT FILLING

½ cup diced cooked chicken or meat
1 diced onion
2 cups diced lettuce
1 cup diced green peppers
Chili powder, salt and pepper to taste

Mix all ingredients together. Place on an oiled skillet and quickly stir-fry for about 2 minutes. Remove from heat.

SERVING

Stack tortillas covered with a cloth napkin. Filling may be served on a divided dish. Serve 3 different fillings and let each person make his own choice. Filling is put on half the tortilla which is then rolled up by hand and eaten. For additional filling recipes see Mexican rolled tortillas, page 109.

Ingredients

3 eggs
1 cup unbleached white flour
2 tablespoons cornstarch
2 cups water
Pinch salt
Filling:
1 cup chopped cooked shrimp or lobster
¾ cup diced celery
¼ cup minced onion
1 tablespoon soy sauce
1 teaspoon sherry
1 teaspoon garlic
¼ cup minced bean sprouts or cabbage
1 teaspoon cornstarch

BATTER

Beat 2 eggs until foamy, then beat in flour, cornstarch, water and salt.

FIRST FRYING

On a heated skillet, pour 1 tablespoon of batter and quickly tilt pan so batter covers bottom of the pan. When edges curl and begin to turn brown, flip egg roll skin onto absorbent towel. Continue until all batter is used. Makes about 28.

SHAPING

Mix 1 egg with filling ingredients. Make into 2" finger shapes and place each on fried side of egg roll skin. Roll up and tuck in ends. Egg rolls may be stored in refrigerator or frozen at this point if desired.

SECOND FRYING

Place egg rolls, seam side down, in 2" of hot oil and brown on both sides.

SERVING

Serve hot with Chinese mustard or sweet and sour sauce.

Index